_f_**P**

OTHER BOOKS BY LEO HINDERY, JR.

The Biggest Game of All: The Inside Strategies, Tactics, and Temperaments That Make Great Dealmakers Great

IT TAKES A CEO

CEO

*

IT'S TIME TO LEAD
WITH INTEGRITY

LEO HINDERY, Jr.

FREE PRESS

NEW YORK   LONDON   TORONTO   SYDNEY

*f*P
FREE PRESS
A Division of Simon & Schuster, Inc.
1230 Avenue of the Americas
New York, NY 10020

FREE PRESS and colophon are trademarks of Simon & Schuster, Inc.

For information about special discounts for bulk purchases,
please contact Simon & Schuster Special Sales:
1-800-456-6798 or business@simonandschuster.com

Manufactured in the United States of America

1   3   5   7   9   10   8   6   4   2

Library of Congress Cataloging-in-Publication Data

Hindery, Leo.
It takes a CEO: it's time to lead with integrity / Leo Hindery.
p.   cm.
Includes bibliographical references and index.
1. Chief executive officers—United States.   2. Chief executive officers—
United States—Professional ethics.   3. Corporations—Corrupt practices—
United States.   4. Social responsibility of business—United States.
5. Industrial relations—United States.   I. Title.
HD38.25.U6H56   2005
658.4'092—dc22   2005051965

ISBN-13: 978-0-7432-6985-8
ISBN-10:   0-7432-6985-3

to my daughter Robin, for her grace and love,
and to my beloved wife Patti,
for her inspiration and support.

ACKNOWLEDGMENTS

I could not have written this book without the support and wisdom of some wonderful friends, first and foremost my collaborator Jeff Cruikshank, who shares my concerns and my passions and who was my partner throughout. Christy Fletcher, my agent on this book and on its predecessor, is much more my muse than my agent, and above all else she is a remarkable friend. And Dominick Anfuso, Editorial Director of Simon & Schuster's Free Press imprint, generously agreed to be my book editor—what a gift to have had his early and enthusiastic support for this project and what a mess it would have been without his editing.

I couldn't (or wouldn't) have started this book, or finished it, without the shared passions and examples, in life and in politics, of the friends who have sustained me for years: Mark Coleman, Tom Daschle, Bob Davis, Dick Gephardt, Anya Hoerburger, Bob Kerrey, David Krone, Justin Lapatine, Mel Levine, Noah Mamet, Kate Michelman, David Mixner, Alan Platt, and Jon Silvan.

CONTENTS

IT TAKES A
CEO

INTRODUCTION
WHAT TAKES A CEO?

I have been the president or CEO of five major media and cable corporations. Based on that experience, I've written a book about corporate deal making *(The Biggest Game of All)*. I've gotten to know lots of movers and shakers: some admirable characters, others less so. I've made a lot of money—for my shareholders and my employees, as well as for myself. And at times, I've pushed my peers in corporate America to think more broadly about things like AIDS, diversity, partner benefits, and other difficult issues.

I'm often asked to speak to corporate and university audiences. Although my stump speech continues to evolve, and although I tailor it to particular audiences, it generally focuses on the need to 1) recognize your responsibilities in life and 2) *act* on those responsibilities. When I get going in front of a crowd, I can generally get that crowd going too.

But it's not an act. I believe every word of it, and I've tried to live it in my own life.

When the title of this book—*It Takes a CEO*—was chosen I realized that some people might misinterpret it. No, the point is *not* that CEOs are all-knowing or all-wise or all-powerful. The point is that CEOs have a special role to play in our society. Because of the way our society is hardwired, there are certain very important things that only a CEO can tackle.

How important are these things, and what's at risk? What's at risk is the entire way of life that we've come to treasure in America, and which people around the world—no matter what they may *say* about us—wish they had for themselves.

WHAT YOU'LL FIND HERE

What you'll find in this book is an analysis of how we've gotten into some of the messes we're in, and also a prescription for getting out of them. I don't intend to pull punches.

For example, a lot of today's crop of CEOs are irresponsible or criminal or both. Some of them—the Kozlowskis, Ebberses, Rigases, Lays, Skillings, and so on—have made headlines with their antics. But there are many more of them out there who are just hunkering down and hoping that their own shenanigans won't turn into tomorrow's headlines. And there's a far bigger bunch who don't have these kinds of skeletons in their closets but unfortunately have nothing to point to on the positive side of the ledger either. When you say to these guys that it takes a CEO, they tend to blink uncomprehendingly and ask, "Well, to do what, exactly?"

In the following pages, we'll look at reasons people should (or shouldn't) go into business in the first place. In my own experience, leading corporations is a tough, lonely job. Pushing corporations and other human organizations in directions they don't necessarily want to go is a long, hard slog. If you do the job right, it may pay you well, but it will definitely cost you dearly. I know this; my first two CEO jobs cost me my marriage.

We'll also look at the overconcentration of power in this country and the negative consequence of that trend. After an early apprenticeship in the natural-resource industry and a stint on Wall Street, I went into the communications and media world, so that's the sector I will focus on to make some of my arguments.

Are you worried that five media companies control more than 80 percent of what's seen in America today? I am.

Are you worried that those companies are engaged in an ethical and aesthetic "race to the bottom"—that is, chasing the highest ratings by sniffing out the lowest common denominator? Are you worried about *Fear Factor* and *The Swan,* and what the networks may be planning next? I am.

Next, we'll look at some executive compensation and corporate-governance issues that CEOs have to think and worry about a lot more. Again, the subtext here is responsibility.

That subtext recurs in the chapters focused on outsourcing and on the corporation's obligation to take care of its employees. No, there are no easy answers to the challenges of competing on a global stage, where some of your faraway competitors couldn't care less about things like exploiting children and despoiling the environment. But the fact that it's hard is no excuse for not trying to deal with the problem. Lots of aspects of business are hard. In theory, at least, that's why CEOs get paid so much.

I also include a chapter that I call "Wal-Mart Nation?" I put the question mark there because the current struggle between Wal-Mart and Costco really speaks to the heart of a terrible dilemma facing our nation. Wal-Mart, in some ways, is the corporate equivalent of *Fear Factor.* Sam Walton's juggernaut has vanquished most of the competition, but the Wal-Mart "win" is not much to be proud of: $9.96 an hour, on average, with one of the most-costly-to-employee health-care "benefits" anywhere. Meanwhile, over at Costco, Jim Sinegal is risking the wrath of Wall Street by trying to do the right thing by his people.

And guess what? His employees know it, and they're trying to do the right thing by him too.

And finally, I include a short chapter called "The CEO Check-list," which is no more or less than standards to which prospective employees should hold their prospective employers. The question they should seek to answer, through this exercise, is, *Is this company good enough for me?*

That may seem like a strange question to be asking in turbulent economic times, when getting and holding on to a job can be a tough challenge. But if *everybody* asked this question—*Is this com-*

pany good enough for me?—Sam Walton's very wealthy heirs and other shareholders wouldn't get away with paying employees just $7.60 an hour.

WHO SHOULD READ THIS BOOK

The preceding quick summary should give you some idea of the kinds of people this book tries to speak to.

Ideally, I'd like to influence some of my fellow CEOs. I have a vision that I savor: the CEOs of this country's thousand largest companies band together, storm Capitol Hill, and declare their collective determination to launch the equivalent of a Marshall Plan to help rescue the U.S. economy and its middle class, just as the original Marshall Plan rescued Europe and its war-torn populations in the wake of World War II. Is this a pipe dream? Maybe. Maybe not.

But by the time you get to be a full-fledged CEO, you're pretty hard to influence. So I really want to influence the next few generations of CEOs in this country. I want to scare certain kinds of young people out of even applying for the job. And I want to encourage other kinds of young people to apply, even while I'm warning them about what they're really getting into.

More broadly, I want to give hope and inspiration to a large and growing group of people who don't currently have much of either. As I write this introduction, the late Ronald Reagan is still being remembered and mourned. In his time as president, Reagan was known and loved for his almost relentless optimism. He talked of cities on hills, of mornings in America, and of a country whose best days were ahead of it. Americans responded to that vision— even Americans who had never before dreamed of signing on with a conservative Republican's agenda.

America's best days *can* be ahead, but not if we continue on the course we are on. We need to change course. We need to steer toward a new shore. That shore is in sight. But it will take a CEO (multiplied by the hundreds and the thousands) to help us get there.

1

THE PROBLEM, AND HOW WE GOT THERE

Today, across the United States, we have something like 12 percent effective unemployment.

Yes, I know that's about three times the reported unemployment rate. But the real numbers are far worse than the reported rates. If you add in all the people who are underemployed or have given up hope of finding work in our economy—including a lot of black males in our cities—the unemployment rate soars. The unemployment rate among black males in New York City, for example, is 50 percent. That's right: *50 percent*.[1] What's more, this is largely "structural" unemployment, which means it's embedded in our system and isn't going to go away with the next uptick in the economy.

My office is in the beautifully refurbished Chrysler Building, in midtown Manhattan. Although I'm only a short cab ride from where most of New York's unemployed live, I could be thousands of miles away from them. Unless I make an effort to bridge that gap, my life is almost completely separate from the lives of the people who live in those communities.

Or is it?

A central premise of this book is that, collectively, we *own* that unemployment—or it owns us. America's corporate leadership, and especially its CEOs, have a special role to play in addressing this great and growing social evil.

When I was a college student in the late 1960s, the unemployment rate among black males in New York was much lower—something like a third of what it is today. Back then, most people thought that the then-prevailing rates of unemployment in the ghetto were scandalously, unacceptably high. Government at every level took bold steps to provide more opportunity for the unemployed. Everyone thought that with a little determined effort, we could make unemployment go away. We could build a "Great Society," as Lyndon Johnson put it. And corporate America played its part—sometimes awkwardly, but with good intentions.

Obviously, the Great Society didn't happen. Instead, we decided to turn our backs on the problem. We couldn't afford both the "guns and butter" that President Johnson promised us, so we embraced the guns. Again, corporate America went with the flow. Our CEOs stopped worrying about what was briefly referred to as "corporate social responsibility" and went back to making money.

The problem doesn't begin and end with employment, unfortunately. Take health insurance. Two or three decades back, nobody talked much about health insurance. For the most part, most people who wanted it were able to get it, at a rate they could more or less afford. Health benefits were taken for granted: *of course* your company offered a relatively generous medical plan, or even several such plans. Not a perfect system, to be sure—among other problems, your health insurance wasn't "portable"—and that's why U.S. presidents since Harry Truman have been arguing in favor of some sort of national health insurance. But all in all, it was a workable system.

Today, according to the latest Kaiser Foundation numbers, there are at least 45 million Americans with no health insurance. In the first two years of this brand-new century, the number of uninsured under the age of sixty-five grew by 3.7 million, or almost 10 percent.[2] These numbers grew in part as a result of the anemic economy, but also—as we will see—mostly as a result of inept government policies and morally bankrupt corporate practices.

Who cares? Well, we all should. When one of these uninsured

people experiences a serious medical problem, emergency or not, he or she heads for the emergency room at the local hospital, which is obligated to provide free care to anyone who needs it.

This is bad medicine, but it's also bad economics. Emergency rooms, which are expensive to operate, should be reserved for actual emergencies. It's no surprise that hospitals are increasingly unwilling to foot the bill. From a social-policy standpoint too, the system is a disaster. Uninsured people rarely visit doctors to keep themselves healthy; that's a luxury reserved for the wealthy and the insured. So the uninsured wait until their medical problem is so far along that they have no choice but to seek help—at which point the problem tends to be hugely expensive to treat, or untreatable.

In either case, somebody pays a very large bill—either in medical care to treat an advanced condition or in lost productivity or both. It may be a company health plan or an already strapped municipal budget, but somebody pays.

In the health-care realm, as in the corporate-social-responsibility realm, our CEOs and other corporate leaders have learned a painful lesson. We can't wish these problems away. We can't wash our hands of them. We own them—or they own us.

THE LARGER IMPLICATIONS OF "EXTREME FIGHTING"

So that's the first premise of this book. I believe, strongly, that this country is facing major challenges and choices. Some of those challenges can't be solved without the direct involvement of America's corporate leadership. It's not a question of those leaders' being "nice guys" or "nice gals." It's a question of their acting in the long-term interests of their organizations and of the nation.

But there's another important premise of this book. In addition to accepting (partial) responsibility for tackling issues like unemployment and health care, our corporate leaders have to take more responsibility for this nation's moral tone and for the quality of our cultural and social discourse. This means different things for different executives, depending on where they and their organizations are today. For some, it means stopping bad things from happening. For others, it means making better things happen.

I was president of TCI—the largest cable operator in the United States—beginning in February 1997. In that capacity, one of my jobs was to pass final judgment on the shows that aired on our numerous cable systems. When I took over at TCI, the company was already involved with a pay-per-view event called "extreme fighting." Basically, extreme fighting involved putting two guys in a Cyclone-fence-enclosed hexagon and having them go at each other until one of the two guys "tapped out."

Biting, kicking, eye gouging, whatever: this was no holds barred. I hated the whole enterprise. I had refused to carry it on the cable systems of InterMedia Partners, which I had started in 1988 and headed before arriving at TCI. Extreme fighting was gladiatorial, perverse—even obscene. So I said, "TCI is out of the extreme fighting business."

In early 1997, I had enough influence over the industry that when I said, "It's off the air at TCI," it wasn't going to happen elsewhere. There was only one practical avenue into the home at that time: through the cable industry. If my company and the larger industry were out, that didn't leave enough homes to be profitable for these guys to invade.

What I didn't fully appreciate at that time was that extreme fighting was an industry, of sorts, and that its backers were absolutely determined to overcome my objections and get into America's homes. So what did they do, in response to my banning of the sport and my condemnation of it as "rule-less"? They came up with something they informally called the "Hindery rules," which they proposed to adopt on a going-forward basis. The Hindery rules boiled down to no eye gouging, no throat jabs, no biting, and no obvious shots to the groin. Apparently, they hoped that by adopting these rules, they could make me and like-minded CEOs back off. Maybe they thought I'd be flattered by having a set of rules named after me. (I wasn't.) In any case, they promulgated these rules, and then they said, "*Now* will you let us come back on?"

I continued to say, "No way. Not on my systems."

I traveled for two years with security. And to make things worse, I began to understand that it wasn't just the fighters and promoters who were angry, it was also the small but passionate *au-*

dience for extreme fighting. They weren't getting their favorite entertainment pumped into their living rooms because of my stubbornness, and they were really, really angry about that.

My response continued to be, *Tough luck.* I was more likely to reroute sewer mains into several million living rooms than to put that garbage on the air, even on a pay-per-view basis. I thought it was wrong, and I thought it was a CEO's job to say so.

I still think so.

THE RACE TO THE BOTTOM

In recent years, America has been engaged in what many have called a "race to the bottom." It's a competitive downward spiral in our economic, cultural, and political lives. It has many manifestations, none of them good.

The shaky state of the national economy has contributed significantly to the swelling ranks of the jobless and uninsured in recent years. (People lose their health insurance both when they get laid off and when their employer goes under.) But in addition, conscious decisions made by people in positions of authority—including both politicians and corporate leaders—have helped bump up those "misery indexes."

For example, U.S. companies have moved aggressively to outsource and "offshore" work to foreign nationals—work that previously was performed by U.S. workers. Some of this offshoring has been a legitimate competitive necessity. But some of it reflects laziness and cowardice on the part of American corporate executives. *Chase the lowest wage rates, wherever they may be in the world,* according to this mind-set. *That's the best short-term thing for my shareholders,* offshoring executives tell themselves, *so it must be the best thing, period.*

Unfortunately—and this is where our politicians have been lazy and cowardly—no one carries this calculation through to its logical extreme. No one figures out the cost to our society of having U.S. workers lose jobs, go on unemployment, get their health care through hospital emergency rooms, and so on. And is my office in the Chrysler Building really that far away from Harlem?

The late Irwin Miller—long the voice and conscience of Columbus, Indiana–based Cummins Inc., which makes diesel engines and related components—used to talk about the need to include in the cost of his company's engines the cost of *cleaning up* after those engines. Doesn't that idea sound quaint today? A corporation acknowledging responsibilities beyond the bare legal minimum?

But it shouldn't sound quaint. Miller was right. If his customers don't pay for the cost of diesel particulates in the air, the rest of us will. Or worse, *nobody* will, and we'll keep on inhaling those particulates indefinitely and pay in far more painful ways. And guess who is more likely to live near a clogged road or freeway: someone like me, or the family of one of those unemployed African-American males mentioned above?

In a survey of 1,500 delegates, mostly top business leaders, attending the World Economic Forum in Davos, Switzerland, in January 2004, fewer than 20 percent of survey respondents said profitability was the most important measure of success. More important, most respondents claimed, were corporate reputation, integrity, and the quality of their products. They may believe it when they say it, but unless they *act* it, it doesn't count.

Extreme fighting was (and unfortunately still is) the epitome in media of the cultural race to the bottom, which in turn is driven by profits, which in turn are driven by ratings or customer acceptance.

Take Janet Jackson's celebrated "wardrobe malfunction" during the 2004 Super Bowl halftime show. In the wake of what turned out to be a public-relations fiasco, CBS issued the following statement:

> CBS deeply regrets the incident that occurred during the Super Bowl halftime show. We attended all rehearsals throughout the week and there was no indication that any such thing would happen. The moment did not conform to CBS broadcast standards and we would like to apologize to anyone who was offended.[3]

Oh, please. Does anyone honestly think that bizarre moment was completely unscripted or unauthorized? As someone who worked in that industry for many years, I sure don't. Why? Because advertisers were paying $1.6 million for a thirty-second spot, and they expected something spectacular.

Because nobody in that entire chain of command, all the way to the top of the CBS pyramid, stood up and said, "It's not going to happen on *my* network." That's exactly what Bill Paley, the founding genius and longtime conscience of CBS, would have said. *Not on my network.*

WHAT WENT WRONG?

What went wrong? How has our society gotten this far off track? There are at least three major contributing factors:

1) *bad corporate leadership,* on the part of our CEOs principally, but also the senior executives (COOs, CFOs, EVPs, and so on) who stand right behind our CEOs,
2) *misguided policies* at the federal level, and
3) *skewed priorities* on the personal level—yours and mine.

Let's look briefly at each of these factors; we'll return to them at greater length in subsequent chapters.

Bad corporate leadership

Leadership is a sacred trust and a privilege. When you head a corporation, you accept—or should accept—all the implications of that trust. When you abuse that trust, there should be consequences. I'm one of those relatively rare executive types who applaud New York Attorney General Eliot Spitzer as he smokes out the bad guys. Corporate bad guys should go to jail.

But bad leadership extends far beyond the small numbers of CEOs who wind up in jail. For example, on May 10, 2004, Citigroup—parent company of Salomon Smith Barney—agreed to pay $2.65 billion to investors who had invested in WorldCom as a result of Jack Grubman's relentlessly cheerful analyses of the shaky telecom giant. (Grubman was Salomon's telecom "expert.") Well, by any reckoning, $2.65 billion is a lot of money. In fact, it was the largest payment ever made by a bank, brokerage firm, or auditor to settle claims made by investors.[4]

Jack Grubman, at his peak, was paid $20 million a year by Salomon to perform his "research" and "analysis." That's a big red flag, right there. There is no analyst in the world who's worth more than $1 million a year. So what did the other $19 million cover?

Could the ugly truth be that it compensated Grubman for his help in landing something like $100 million in investment-banking work from WorldCom? Perhaps there were other things at work—like the fact that Grubman raised his research rating of AT&T at an especially timely juncture, after Weill had requested Grubman to "take a fresh look" at the stock. And the fact that, after Grubman reportedly asked Weill to pull some strings to get Grubman's twins into a highly competitive Manhattan preschool, the twins were duly admitted to the school, which also happened to receive a $1 million donation from Citigroup.

With Spitzer nipping at his heels, Grubman agreed to pay a $15 million fine and accepted a lifetime banishment from the securities industry.[5] Poor guy—nine months' pay down the drain, and no more time at the trough!

But what of Sandy Weill—the other guy in the middle of this mess, and, as the CEO, the person ultimately responsible for his company's paying a fine bigger than the total annual expenditures of twelve of the fifty states?[6,7] Well, he still gets the best tables at New York restaurants, and he still relishes his role as senior corporate statesman about town.

Frankly, Weill deserves a lifetime banishment from positions of corporate leadership. And he should be compelled to give back some of his enormous past compensation ($30.7 million in FY 2003 alone, according to *Forbes*).

The only risk in focusing on the most obvious cases—the felons and the corrupt peacocks—is that other, less conspicuous characters may escape detection and punishment. Obviously, there are sins of commission: the kinds of criminal activities that the Eliot Spitzers of the world are going after. But there are also sins of omission: all those things a responsible CEO *could* do to make his or her company stronger, and the lives of his or her employees better, but opts not to.

Misguided federal policies

For much of the last quarter century, our federal government has frequently made matters worse as it's tried to make them better. Let's look first at a fairly noncontroversial manifestation of this phenomenon: how our government has dealt with the challenge of overcapacity. If you really sit down and pick apart what's wrong with the U.S. auto industry, the airlines, and the telecom sector, you quickly come to the realization that we have way too much capacity—too many production facilities, too many seats, too much cable, and so on.

Overcapacity is hard to spot, but its effects are not. It's like a flesh-eating bacterium, first ravaging balance sheets and profit-and-loss statements, then gnawing away at employment, and finally hurting the lending institutions that stand behind all that overcapacity. Look at the sad case of Japan. At the beginning of the 1990s, the formerly vaunted Japanese economy (remember Ezra F. Vogel's 1979 classic, *Japan as Number 1?*) began to feel the results of its own extreme structural overcapacity. The Nikkei plunged, and it remained depressed for almost fifteen years.

The U.S. economy, which consistently demonstrates an astounding resiliency, can generally overcome any dislocations it encounters. But no economy—not even ours—can accommodate widespread overcapacity. About the best thing you can do, when staring down the gun barrel of this threat, is 1) stimulate consumption, and 2) take the necessary steps to avoid the creation of even more unproductive capacity.

So what does our government do? First, through the Federal Reserve—ostensibly an independent body, but increasingly responsive in recent years to the whims of the White House—it cuts interest rates, which puts money into the hands of corporations, which are tempted to build even more capacity. Fortunately, many have resisted that temptation, perhaps taking their cue from the commercial real-estate sector, which—having gotten whacked as a result of having brought way too much capacity on line in the late 1980s—wisely declined to make the same mistake a decade later.

Sure, low interest rates help consumers control the cost of their debt. But that's just an accidental benefit for individuals who are owned by their credit-card debt. The *real* goal of this monetarist policy, believe it or not, is to encourage corporations *to invest in new capacity.*

Second, our government persists in designing tax cuts for people in the higher income brackets. To put it bluntly, *tax cuts for rich people only make rich people richer.* Giving more money to people who are already in full-consumption mode—and therefore are unlikely to spend more—is bad economics, not to mention an affront to the rest of society. The scheduled complete elimination of the estate tax is an absolutely shameful extension of this warped, counterproductive tax policy. We need to go in *exactly the opposite direction.* We need to put more money in the hands of the people who absolutely need to spend it; that will help consumption go up. Keep capacity down; push consumption up. Even a semiretired media exec understands that much about economics.

Some economists have argued that the "cruelest tax" is inflation. That's the kind of argument made by someone who's never been unemployed. The cruelest tax is unemployment. Since the beginning of this century, this nation has permanently lost between 2.3 million and 3 million jobs to outsourcing. (The figure tends to bounce around, depending on who you listen to.) Certainly under the recent Republican administration—but also dating back into the Clinton years, and before that in the Bush I and Reagan administrations—our federal government has adopted a relentlessly uncritical probusiness stance. The theory is that free trade will set us free.

It hasn't worked. U.S. employers simply cannot compete against the combination of child labor, substandard compensation, few or no employee benefits, and zero-to-low environmental standards at overseas sources of production.

Although he is far from alone in this, the current President Bush has demonstrated an amazing insensitivity to those millions of lost jobs. He has talked about how "dislocations" are inevitable and—

in the long run—good for the economy. He has talked about how health spas are a growing sector of the economy, where the "dislocated" might want to start their second (or third or fourth) careers.

Sorry. We can, and must, do better.

Skewed personal priorities

Now we need to spread the blame a little more broadly, extending it to you and to me—to all of us.

We're greedy. We overconsume.

Have you visited a new and upscale suburban housing development recently? There's an obligatory feature in new and upscale houses: the "great room"—a cavernous chamber designed to make the house's owner feel wealthy and important, like a feudal lord.

Or if you live in an established neighborhood, try to find a house that hasn't gotten bigger in recent years. The added wing. The enclosed porch. The attached garage that has been transformed into a playroom. Our families aren't getting bigger—in fact, they're getting smaller, year by year—but we seem to need more and more room to spread out in.

That's in part because *we're* getting bigger. The average weight of Americans aged twenty-five to thirty in the mid-1980s was 161 pounds. Ten years later, the average weight in that same age group was 171 pounds.[8]

We persist in driving big cars that waste gas. We particularly like trucks (or disguised trucks, like SUVs). As a result, despite enormous technological advances, we use gasoline less efficiently than we did a decade and a half ago. "The total fleet fuel economy peaked in 1987 at 26.2 mpg when light trucks made up a mere 28.1 percent of the market," notes one government agency. "By 2001, with light trucks making up 46.7 percent of the market, total fleet fuel economy fell to 24.4 mpg. Currently, light trucks make up more than 50 percent of new vehicle sales."[9]

Meanwhile, we engage in the kinds of selfish economic behaviors that help us only a little but hurt American workers a lot. Are you more likely to buy an American-made sweatshirt at that store on Main Street for thirty bucks, or drive that SUV out to Wal-Mart on the edge of town and spend twenty bucks on a sweatshirt made in China? If you take the latter course, you benefit your own budget a little, but the ruins of the domestic textile industry take another hit.

A few years back, Robert D. Putnam wrote a compelling book called *Bowling Alone,* the premise of which was that social bonds and civic engagement have declined precipitously in the United States over the past few decades. In explaining this phenomenon, Putnam pointed to multiple factors: time pressures, economic stress, residential mobility, the influence of television, and so on.[10] It was a sobering litany, underscoring how much ground we have to recapture before we even begin to think about gaining new ground.

It is no accident that two of our oldest states—Massachusetts and Virginia—are technically not states at all but "commonwealths." A great word, and a great concept: the *common wealth.* The green space in the middle of Boston is referred to as Boston Common because it was originally grazing land for cattle owned in common by the settlers. When those early New Englanders had to put up a barn, they had a barn raising, and people came from miles around to pitch in—confident that when *they* needed help, their neighbors would be there for them.

Would you be there for your neighbors? Would they be there for you? In a global economy, who *are* your neighbors?

So What Are We Supposed to Do?

Books that are 99 percent catalogues of evil and only 1 percent *solutions* to those evils aren't particularly useful. In this book, I intend to devote as much space as possible to prescriptions. The following pages sketch out a few of the prescriptions that will recur throughout subsequent chapters, using the same three-part framework introduced above: business leaders, the government, and the rest of us.

What CEOs have to do

CEOs have to take responsibility for their actions. CEOs have to show some guts and demonstrate some long-range vision. In the realm of job creation, wages, and benefits, this means taking concerted actions to defend the American workforce. In the media realm, this means (among other things) not putting junk like extreme fighting or *Fear Factor* or *The Swan* on the air. This will not be easy. When I thumbed my nose at the extreme-fighting crowd, I was in a strong position. Because of the state of technology and the way the cable industry was structured at that time, there was basically only one pipeline into the living room, and I substantially influenced that pipeline. It was almost impossible for someone to come along behind me and tell the extreme-fighting crowd, "Hey, I'll take your garbage, happily!"

That is no longer true. The woman who recently took over the troubled ABC network, Ann Sweeney, is an outstanding media executive. She used to run the Disney Channel; now she's attempting to turn around ABC. In addition to being a topflight television executive, she's a seriously good mother and also a thoughtful person who is committed to women's issues and other important causes.

Nevertheless, Sweeney is working against long odds. She needs to find ways to break the downward spiral that Fox Network initiated a few years back, with its degrading reality programming. Both the economics of production (reality TV is cheap) and the proliferation of alternatives are working against her, in ways that they weren't even a decade ago. But she has to try. It takes a CEO. And to extrapolate more broadly, CEOs across this country need to find ways to break our downward spirals and interrupt the race to the bottom.

We have just concluded an election season, resulting in the reelection of George W. Bush. No matter what our partisan preferences, here's one thing we should all wish for the president: less stuff on his plate, and more stuff on the plates of the CEO community.

What do I mean by this? What we've really done, through our recent political process, is elect a president of the world (even if the rest of the world hates to hear it put that way). Now we will demand that he operate effectively on that level, focusing on big-picture issues. But the fact is, he's not going to have that luxury, because he's going to have to address all those issues on which the corporate sector has simply abdicated responsibility—the 45 mil-

lion people with no health insurance, the outsourcing, the indecency on the airwaves, the media consolidation, the decision about
whether to expense options or put them through the balance sheet,
and so on, and so on. It will not matter if President Bush (or his successor) tries to sidestep these tough issues; eventually, they will
catch up with him and bedevil him.

Just as they will bedevil us.

It takes a CEO. It's not a case of hubris or misplaced pride. The
CEO's job touches on three constituencies: employees, shareholders, and community. It touches on them automatically, and un-
avoidably. The bigger your company, the bigger each of those
constituencies. And when you get to the size of a Fortune 1000
company, your community is arguably the nation.

A few years back, I had a version of this conversation with
Gerry Levin, who recently retired as the head of Time Warner.
Among the divisions in Levin's former empire was Interscope
Records—which put out rap records that advocated the killing of
cops—and another division was the publisher of one of Madonna's
more reprehensible picture books. When I challenged him about
his company's involvement in these activities, Levin first invoked
the First Amendment. After exhausting the free-speech argument,
he fell back on the great corporate cop-out: maximizing shareholder wealth. But it's simply not good enough for our CEOs to
draw their circles of responsibility so tightly, worrying only about
the needs of their shareholders.

The debate continues, at Time Warner and elsewhere.[11] I hope
that in the long run, the broader view of corporate responsibility
prevails. I hope that our corporate leaders, either individually or
collectively, will chart out a course of action that meets the needs of
all their constituencies.

Sometimes CEOs adopt a philosophical approach to explain
their inaction. "It's not appropriate for me to throw my weight
around in the social arena," they say. "It's not appropriate for me
to commit my company to a social, economic, or political agenda.
These are issues best left to the democratic process."

The appropriate response is "If not you, who?" Remember
when President Nixon made his overture to China? No liberal

politician would have dared to cozy up to the Red Chinese government, as it was universally referred to in the United States at the
time. It was too risky for a Democrat. It took a Republican. Well,
who's going to make similarly bold departures on the citizen and
worker home fronts? Who's going to draw the line when someone
proposes yet another race to the bottom?

It takes a CEO.

What the government has to do

In the near term, the government (primarily at the federal level,
but also to some extent at the state and local levels) has to make up
for the failings of our CEO community. Currently, several more
states—Washington and Oregon among them—are considering
following the New York legislature's lead in banning extreme fighting. "What kind of society are we becoming?" asked one state senator from Washington rhetorically. "It's almost as if we're
throwing people to the tigers in the amphitheater in Rome." [12] Arizona Senator John McCain—a boxer in his days at the Naval Academy, and a boxing aficionado ever since—deserves credit for his
tireless crusade against extreme fighting.

In the longer term, the government has to work with the CEO
community (and vice versa) in ways that benefit American workers—starting at home, but especially in the realm of international
competition. An individual CEO, or even a group of CEOs, can't
wrestle with the WTO about the rules of competition on a global
scale. That's the government's job. But up to that point, it's every
CEO's job, on a daily basis, to position his or her company so that
the government isn't compelled to fight uphill every step of the way.

My fellow CEOs should always keep in mind that if we don't
do it ourselves, the government will do it for us—or to us. And the
problem with that solution, of course, is that the government
paints with a roller, when what's usually needed is a much smaller
and more flexible paintbrush.

What the rest of us have to do

In *Bowling Alone,* Robert Putnam waits until his very last
chapter to start suggesting what we're supposed to do about our

sense of being disconnected from one another. His prescriptions range from the mundane (get more involved in civic work) to the lofty (agitate for large-scale urban planning that will minimize the atomization of the culture).

Unlike Putnam's, this book is primarily about CEOs: what they can and can't do, and what they should and shouldn't do. For that reason, I won't spend much time on Putnam's turf. But heading into our subsequent chapters, I will simply reiterate that we're all in this together. We can't do what needs to be done without the inspired leadership of the CEO community. And they can't do what needs to be done without our support—yours and mine.

2

THE FEW. THE PROUD. THE BRAVE.

Who should become a CEO, and why? Who among the junior ranks of today's executive corps should angle for the job? How should students getting out of business schools think about the responsibilities of the corner office?

TOUGH AT THE TOP

One way to start to answer those questions is to ask today's CEOs what they think. In October 2003, *The Economist* published what it called a "survey of corporate leadership."[1] The surveyors asked a group of high-level executives a series of questions in the middle months of 2003. Following are some of the more interesting findings:

- CEOs are "now expected to take personal responsibility for [their companies'] fortunes as never before."
- The level of external scrutiny is "far beyond anything a corporate leader would have been subjected to in the past."
- People have "come to expect more from corporate leaders."
- A July 2002 poll suggested that "only 23 percent of Americans thought the bosses of large corporations could be trusted."

- Corporate boards are becoming increasingly "trigger-happy," meaning that they're more likely to dump their CEO faster. "A CEO appointed between 1990 and 1996 was three times more likely to be fired than one appointed before 1980."
- "A sacked CEO . . . may be literally unemployable."
- And finally, in its list of "ten commandments for successful leaders," *The Economist* put "a sound ethical compass" as Commandment 1: "If the boss's values are undemanding, the company's will also be wobbly. . . . Good people do not like working for organizations whose values they mistrust. But ethical values are difficult to acquire on demand, in middle life."

As you read the rest of this chapter, keep Commandment 1 in mind. If you're an aspiring CEO, do you possess that "sound ethical compass"? If you're thinking about joining or investing in a particular company, do you have confidence that there's such a compass at work in the corner office?

If not, maybe you need a new plan.

THE CEO AS MARINE

The Marine Corps uses the phrase "the few, the proud, the Marines" in its recruiting drives. It's a great slogan because, in a very concise way, it gets a lot of work done.

First, it appeals to our sense of wanting to belong to an exclusive group. *The few.* Why would you want to join any other kind of group, when you can belong to an elite?

Second, it describes us in relation to some kind of tradition. *The proud.* We are part of something bigger than ourselves— something that stretches over time, and which creates expectations in us, and for us.

And finally, it prescribes an outlook and a pattern of behavior. *The brave.* It describes what will be expected of us, if we are among the few and the proud. And, of course, it reinforces that sense of being among the elite. We know that everybody is brave. We'd like to think that we're among that small group of people who have the courage of their convictions—who will stand up for what's right in the face of disapproval or even a threat to one's career.

Why this focus on elites, pride, and courage? Because these traits characterize an effective CEO just as much as they describe a member of the U.S. Marine Corps. An elite? Absolutely. As a CEO, you've got more money, perks, and power than the next hundred people put together—or perhaps more than the next three hundred people put together.

Pride? You can't do the job without taking pride in it. Effective CEOs come to understand their organizations in their bones, and—assuming they're with a good enterprise—take great pride in them. Conversely, a talented person won't give up his or her life to an undeserving organization just for the money and access to the corporate jet. We want to belong to something bigger *and better* than ourselves. We are all on a search for meaning in our lives, and we want to affiliate with great institutions. True, we live in a cynical age, and most people don't wear this kind of loyalty on their sleeves anymore. But it's there, all the same, and CEOs want to feel it, and live it.

And by the way, effective CEOs understand that everyone else in the organization wants to feel this degree of loyalty as well.

Effective CEOs also demonstrate great courage: they are the brave. This courage shows up in all kinds of ways—some dramatic, some almost invisible. Perhaps you recall when Jim Burke of Johnson & Johnson pulled one of his company's bread-and-butter products, Tylenol, off the market in response to a series of deaths caused by product tampering. That was dramatic, to say the least. It had to be done, and Burke did it.

But in many cases, when things aren't going so well, an effective CEO shows great courage just by getting out of bed in the morning. A friend of mine told me about a conversation he once had with Don Tyson—the entrepreneur who turned an Arkansas chicken farm into a $25 billion conglomerate. My friend asked Tyson if he had found a particular business decision difficult. "Hell, no," Tyson growled in response. "That was easy. What's hard is just waking up every morning, knowing that a hundred thousand people are depending on you to do the right thing by them, time after time after time. *That's* hard!"

Tyson might have also mentioned all the other people who depend, in turn, on those hundred thousand to feed, clothe, house, and educate them. To shoulder such a responsibility every day takes courage.

WHO SHOULD BECOME A CEO?

At the risk of stating the obvious, only elite people should belong to an elite.

But by "elite," I don't mean the sort of blue-blood, silver-spoon, inherited-wealth kind of elite that used to characterize the upper echelons of business. Instead, I mean an elite of the mind and the heart—an elite of people who bring to the table the kind of judgment that enables them to do the right thing, time after time after time.

Maybe the simplest way of illustrating this is to point to the nonelite types who have made many headlines in recent years—the leaders of companies like WorldCom, Enron, Global Crossing, and many others. When circumstances called upon them to do the right thing, they did the wrong thing, time after time after time.

An elite character is particularly important because business is such a wide-open universe. It's a frontier—always changing, always consuming itself, always moving on to the next thing. It's a universe of "creative destruction," as Harvard economist Joseph Schumpeter used to put it. There aren't a lot of fixed points; therefore, you need to bring along your own moral compass. Sure, there are all kinds of watchdogs out there: the stock exchanges, the SEC, shareholders, the media, environmental groups, labor unions, city hall—you name it. But the truth is that on the cutting edge of business, at its upper reaches, you (as the CEO) are effectively all by yourself. You're essentially making it up as you go along. You're using that moral compass to feel your way toward the right answers.

Journalism presents an interesting contrast. Compared to running a company, practicing journalism is a relatively straightforward profession. It presents what the financial community calls "bright lines" to its practitioners. Journalists are not supposed to plagiarize or lie or betray their sources. They're supposed to *try* to get the story right—who, what, when, where, why—but they're not going to be fined or jailed if they get the story wrong. In England, you can get convicted of libel if a court decides that you simply didn't try hard enough to get the story right, and sometimes just for getting the story wrong. But in the United States—thanks to the determination of the Founding Fathers to keep the Fourth Estate hard on the heels of government—you generally can't get convicted of libel unless it can be proved that you *knew* you had the story wrong and went ahead and printed it (or broadcast it) anyway.

So journalism, by this measure, is an uncomplicated profession. The signposts are in plain sight.

How about medicine? Well, to be sure, it's increasingly difficult to run a profitable practice in a managed-care environment, and brain surgery is the definition of difficult. But in terms of professional obligations, the brain surgeon too has the benefit of bright lines, laid down in front of him or her. He or she has to observe the main thrust of the Hippocratic oath—*Do no harm*—admit when he or she doesn't know something, and respect the patient's privacy.[2] Again, pretty straightforward.

Law? My longtime friend, partner, and lawyer Mark Coleman won't approve of this analysis of his trade. But in fact, he and his professional peers have a clear standard (and only one standard) to observe: *Represent your clients' interests over your own.*

Veterinarians? *Cause no prolonged suffering.*

Air traffic controllers? *Get them up safely, and then get them back down safely.*

And so on, and so on.

The point here, again, is that a CEO has no similar bright lines to follow. At moments of doubt, crisis, and stress, with a hundred thousand people counting on your judgment, there's no three-word phrase to fall back on. You have to look inside yourself.

And when you do, you'd better find something there. When it comes to making the really tough decisions that CEOs are called upon to make—relocating jobs, changing employee benefits, doing something that's right even if it threatens the bottom line—you had better have a moral compass that you can count on.

WHAT'S INSIDE OF YOU?

We've already talked about the moral compass of the leaders at WorldCom, Enron, and so forth. But maybe that's yesterday's news. Maybe we should be asking, What about tomorrow's corporate leaders? What's the state of their moral compass?

The news is not all good.

I enrolled at the Stanford Business School in the fall of 1969. That was the same year that Thomas W. Harrell, a faculty member with an expertise in applied psychology, started his locally famous survey of the school's incoming students. Basically, it asked a series of megaquestions: Why are you here? What are you trying to accomplish?

Well, my classmates and I were a number of different things, but we weren't stupid. Harrell's questionnaire just about cried out for certain kinds of answers. Why are you here? *I'm here to learn the skills required to save the world.* What do you want to accomplish, in the long term? *I want to save the world, using my newly acquired skills.* As I recall, we were also interviewed two years later, as we were about to leave Stanford, so that Harrell could gauge how our experiences at Stanford had changed our perspectives. I'm sure we answered more or less in the same vein: saving the world and so on.

Were we cynical? Probably we were, to some extent. And we were also at the tail end of those generations that felt as though they should figure out what the relevant authority figures wanted to hear and give it to them. At the same time, there was also a certain amount of idealism fueling our calculated, save-the-world answers. Remember, this was the fall of 1969. Much of urban America had been set afire over the previous two summers. In fact, the world *needed* to be saved. It was already becoming clear that government was not the answer to all of society's problems. Surely, experts in management could play their part. We could do well *and* do good.

Life takes its mysterious twists and turns. Thirty years later, in the late 1990s, I found myself on the Stanford Business School's Advisory Council. In that capacity, we council members were advised of the results of that year's student survey.[3] For the first time ever, a majority of the incoming students came right out and said the unmentionable: *I'm here to make money. I'm not looking to save the world; I'm looking to get rich.*

Remember that this was just about at the peak of the dotcom bubble. Those were strange times. Admitted students were failing to show up at orientation because (as it later turned out) they had gotten an offer from some hot local start-up. Enrolled students were dropping out after a year—or even after a few months—to pursue their entrepreneurial dreams. Many got rich.

Because of Stanford's proximity to Silicon Valley—an offspring of Stanford's graduate schools of engineering and business—the Stanford Business School's student ranks were particularly vulnerable to raids by start-ups. My understanding is that the same sorts of excesses were happening at the Harvard Business School and other top-tier B-schools in this time period. But that doesn't make the individual occurrences any less objectionable. These were young adults who had accepted a responsibility by taking a much-coveted slot at a great school and then thrown it overboard in favor of what they took to be a better offer.

The ones who showed up for orientation and stayed on campus at least long enough to complete the student survey rounded out a troubling picture. Here were some of the world's most talented young people declaring in writing that they really only aspired to get rich. They didn't seem to have a sense that there was a world out there that might need something far better from them.

To me, it's troubling to hear people celebrate the so-called greatest generation, as Tom Brokaw referred to the World War II–era age cohort in his book of the same name. Such a broad-brush description of a huge group of disparate people almost *has* to be wrong. So I'm on thin ice when I begin to imply that my generation worried more about social responsibility than did the generation that was pursuing its dreams during the dotcom craze. One thing, at least, is certain: the collapse of the dotcom economy, starting in the summer and fall of 2000, forced a lot of these same young people to reexamine their dreams and look inside themselves. Maybe that's the silver lining to the dotcom cloud.

In the wake of the corporate scandals that began surfacing about this same time, several leading business schools announced plans to incorporate new ethics modules into their curriculum. Instead of the old Enron cases—in which that Houston-based energy trader looks like a brilliantly designed and managed company— students will be exposed to new cases about Enron. (The old Enron cases are no longer in the active files.) Well, ethics modules aren't necessarily a waste of time. But they aren't going to get through to the students who most need some remedial values work—the ones who are only there to get rich. Those young people, unfortunately, will view their ethics module as instruction in how not to get caught.

WHO SHOULD *NOT* BECOME A CEO?

John McPhee, the author of a number of endlessly interesting non-fiction books on unlikely topics, was once asked at an MIT forum about what kind of person should become a writer. "If you can imagine being anything else," he replied, "be that instead. Don't be a writer."

What McPhee was saying, in so many words, was that being a professional writer was a tough, demanding, grind-you-down kind of job. He was saying that a writer needs certain kinds of inner resources that can't be willed into existence, purchased online, or faked. Those resources have to be in place, ready to be called upon, or the writer can't succeed.

The same is true for a CEO. If you think you can acquire grit, determination, empathy, vision, pride, and courage *after* you get the top job, you are deluding yourself. This is why you need to look inside yourself. Do you see a person who is prepared to take responsibility for hundreds, thousands, or tens of thousands of people's lives? If not, maybe you should think about another line of work.

Who shouldn't be a CEO? There was one specific answer in *USA Today,* not so long ago, in a story about John Rigas, the now-disgraced former head of Adelphia Communications.[4] Rigas was the child of immigrants; he briefly worked in his parents' short-order restaurant before setting his sights higher. After getting a degree from Rensselaer Polytechnic Institute, he began working at a Sylvania television-tube plant. In his spare time, he bought a broken-down movie theater in the small Pennsylvania town of Coudersport. Correctly foreseeing the future of entertainment in the United States, he bought the Coudersport cable franchise in 1952 and in subsequent decades parlayed that tiny toehold into the nation's sixth-largest cable operator. In 2001, he was inducted into the Cable Television Hall of Fame.

But in the spring of 2002, misdeeds began to surface at Adelphia—including corporate guaranties of some $2.3 billion in loans to Rigas and his family members. The prosecutor in the case later said that the Rigases had "used Adelphia as a private piggy bank." And in July 2004, Rigas and one of his sons, Timothy, were found guilty of multiple counts of bank fraud and securities fraud.

To some extent, the collapse of Adelphia's house of cards had strong parallels to WorldCom's implosion. In both cases, there *was* a good business there—an effective organization selling a useful product or service to people who were willing to pay for it. But as at WorldCom, a string of high-priced acquisitions—intended to keep Adelphia in a fast-moving game—led to a mountain of debt (some $13 billion) that had to be serviced. As investor confidence sagged, and the stock price started to sink, and bankers started pointing to loan covenants that called for a specific level of collateralization, Adelphia had more and more trouble staying ahead of its mountain.

So, OK, you make a bad bet on the economy, you get into trouble, and you (and your company and its employees) wind up paying a price. That's forgivable, if not admirable. (You're just an ineffective CEO, not a reprehensible CEO.) What's *not* forgivable is letting your company pay the bills run up by your private and unrelated businesses, pay for family vacations and personal memberships in country clubs, and underwrite the art film that one of your family members has decided to make. What's *not* forgivable is inflating your customer base to make the numbers look better—in order to hoodwink the analysts into writing better reports on your company—or setting up kickbacks with suppliers to provide another way of sweetening the corporate numbers.

All of this happened at Adelphia, and it all amounts to absolutely incontrovertible evidence that John Rigas was never cut out to be a CEO.

Nor was Dennis Kozlowski, the potentate of Tyco International. In June 2005, after a retrial, Kozlowski was convicted of looting nearly $600 million from Tyco—another good company that deserved a good leader. Among the damning evidence that prosecutors relied on to expose Kozlowski's opulent lifestyle (at Tyco's expense) was the fact that he had his company pay half of the $2.1 million it cost to mount a weeklong fortieth birthday party in Sardinia for his girlfriend-cum-wife, buy a $6,000 shower curtain for his New York apartment, and hire a naval architect to help him build a 150-foot yacht.[5]

According to published accounts, Kozlowski was an objectionable character dating back all the way to his days at Seton Hall. He was a screamer and yeller. The things that put him in line to become a CEO—his raw, naked aggression; his self-promotion—were the very things that should have *disqualified* him.

Ken Lay, over at Enron? Well, it looks as if the criminal justice system is finally catching up with him. His defense, according to published accounts, is that he had *no idea* what the evil wizards below him in the organization were doing. Not good enough!

When you review this sorry list—which could be vastly extended—it is stunning to see the cavalier way that this crop of wayward CEOs has treated other people's money. Whatever happened to the concept of stewardship—of protecting something that has been entrusted to you, as a leader?

Back in 1988, I started my own cable company as a private venture, just as John Rigas did in his own way. In my case, I raised $190 million of equity from thirteen investors. The one investment that I will always remember, and the one that most humbled me, was the $2.5 million put up by the Bank of Hawaii with the approval of its then newly named vice chairman, Jack Tsui. Tsui, whom I had not known before, listened to a cold pitch from me, believed in me and my business concept, and made the *first-ever* private equity investment by the Bank of Hawaii.

From that day forward, I lived in complete dread of losing the bank's money. The simple fact was that if I went down, I was very likely going to take Tsui's reputation (and maybe his career) down a peg or two as well.

Talk about a motivator! Like Don Tyson, I used to wake up in the morning terrified of letting people down. Pretty soon, I had a lot of people on the payroll—some 3,000 of them at InterMedia, and later 35,000 at TCI—and that was another great motivator. I never wanted to go to investors or shareholders and tell them I'd stumbled. And I certainly never wanted to walk onto a parking lot full of employees and tell them that I'd let them down. All of that scared me to death. That's why I earned myself my seven-day-a-week reputation. I was terrified of letting people down, especially my employees. I suddenly had a mistress: work. And, as noted previously, she cost me my marriage.

I put everything through that screen of terror. Just by the nature of my industry, the cable industry, I operated in a highly leveraged environment. (It was grow or die, and the best way to grow was to use leverage to consolidate markets and gobble up systems—a world that John Rigas and Bernie Ebbers understood well.) When Congress passed the 1992 Cable Act, which reregulated the cable industry, that legislation cost us an absolute ton of revenues, at a point when we didn't have a lot of revenues to give away. I remember that my reaction was, again, terror: "Are you *kidding* me? You're changing the rules of the game *after* I've put all my chips down?"

In February 1997, when I took over TCI, the company had seven times indebtedness and was trading at six times cash flow. We were essentially broke. We were nothing special: the whole industry was broke. I flew 900,000 air miles in 2.5 years. I wanted to be *everywhere*. Why? I was afraid of my employees' losing their jobs. I was afraid that their 401(k)s would become worthless. I was afraid I would ruin the lives not only of all those people on my payroll, but also of all those people who *depended* on the people on my payroll.

And that's what is so loathsome about the stories coming out of Adelphia, Tyco, WorldCom, and elsewhere. The leaders of those companies simply screwed the people under them, and *they don't care*. For understandable reasons, like trying to hang on to their money and stay out of jail, they'll dispute the specific things they're accused of, while they're looking to plea-bargain. But almost without exception, they show no contrition. They demonstrate no compassion for the innocent victims whose lives they've wrecked.

These guys are, or appear to be, above it all. They're oblivious. Or worse, they understand full well what they've done, and they still don't care. Ken Lay simply doesn't care that he destroyed his workers. He and his cronies cooked up inducements for the nonexecutives on the payroll to buy Enron stock. Then they set up mechanisms making it difficult for those people to get out of their Enron holdings—even while they themselves were frantically selling off their own Enron stock.

Sometimes it's helpful for CEOs to put a face, and a name, in the very front of their brains when they are contemplating some business move that might affect their employees adversely. Well, here's one for Ken Lay: Janice Farmer, sixty-one, a retired Enron worker who was living in Orlando when the Enron scam unraveled and her portfolio (mainly Enron stock) shrank from $700,000 to $20,418. "It may be too late for you to help me," Farmer told a Senate panel in late 2001. "It is not too late for you to take some action to make sure this does not happen to anyone else again."[6]

You could find similar victims in each of these cases. Take Tyco: maybe Dennis Koslowski shouldn't be punished for having a ridiculous, extravagant bash for his girlfriend on Sardinia, featuring an ice replica of Michelangelo's David peeing vodka and a huge birthday cake shaped like a woman with sparklers in her breasts. Let his stockholders and their lawyers worry about that. Kozlowski should be punished because he destroyed 401(k)s, and jobs, and *lives*.

WHERE DOES IT START?

If you're a potential CEO, you need to know going into your job that it carries with it some important ethical obligations. There's a price you pay—or should pay—for never having to stand in line at the airport for a cab, but instead having that polite guy with the sign meet you down by the baggage carousel, grab your bags, and whisk you off to that really nice hotel overlooking the harbor. That's what's so troubling about the results of that poll of the Stanford Business School class of 1999. Are they prepared to pay a price, in the sense of seeing a world that's bigger than themselves? Will they even see those responsibilities when they arise? Or will they be seduced by the benefits and perks?

Even as we focus on the CEO, we shouldn't let anyone else on the ladder of corporate responsibility off the hook. If you don't care about people, that lack of empathy didn't start when you moved into the corner office. You *always* had a piece missing.

The responsibility to be proud and courageous starts early in your career, long before you acquire real power. This may take the form of whistle-blowing, whether internal or external. If you're in the internal audit department at WorldCom, for example, you simply have to blow the whistle on the improper use of accruals and the inappropriate capitalization of operating costs. You have an *absolute responsibility* to speak up. That's exactly what happened at WorldCom, and that's one reason why the scams at that company eventually unraveled. An insider took a risk and took responsibility.

Later in your career, taking responsibility may mean standing up to the boss and pointing out the negative human impacts of one course of action versus another. The HR group almost certainly was not in the room when Enron's leaders were discussing the impact of their shenanigans on the company's retirement plans.

Truth in advertising? That's *your* job, even if you're only a lower-level marketing type. Health standards in the plant? Again, that's *your* job, even if you just got your first pair of protective eyewear and you're not exactly sure what you're talking about as you look across that assembly line.

The head of programming at CBS has an obligation not to put junk on the air. The person who decides that there will or won't be a particular employee benefit at Wal-Mart has an obligation to share the profits of the organization with those who generate the profits.

What are the CEO's responsibilities toward the people down the ladder, especially in the realm of setting standards of responsibility? Think about those young people from Stanford (and, presumably, other top business schools as well) as they come into your organization. They need to be set on the right path. When they hit your doorstep, they're as impressionable as they will ever be.

And that's precisely the point when you have to take them by surprise. It's the juncture when you absolutely have to sit them down and say, "Look, there's an ethical, political, moral aspect to almost all of what you're doing here. And you're going to be confronted with challenges at every step of your career, so you'd better know those challenges are coming. Better yet, you should go seek them out while they're still smaller and more manageable."

You have to make it clear that good habits are set early. If they wait until they're fifty years old to worry about these issues, they'll be in trouble.

And then, of course, having put them on the right path, you have to be prepared to listen to what they tell you—even the bad news. "Ken Lay's failure was that he just wanted to hear good news," according to Sherron Watkins, the so-called Enron whistle-blower. "Leaders have to be able to have their ear attuned to bad news, too."[7] Leaders have to have their ears *especially* attuned to the bad news.

TOUGH AT THE BOTTOM TOO

We opened this chapter with the findings of a poll from *The Economist* magazine. The article was entitled "Tough at the Top."

It *is* tough at the top. Especially with the passage of Sarbanes-Oxley, CEOs have to (literally) sign on the dotted line, attesting to the truthfulness of their numbers. They are intensely scrutinized— although when a tough decision has to be made, they'll be all by themselves. People expect more from the CEO, at the same time that they trust him or her less. And the moral compass referred to throughout this chapter is not a nice-to-have for the CEO; it's an absolute necessity for keeping the organization from being "wobbly," and for making it a place where people are proud to work and a company in which investors are proud to invest.

So, yes, it's tough at the top. But it's far tougher at the bottom. Eight months after the results of the above-cited survey were published, *The Economist* came out with a second survey, entitled "Tough at the Bottom." This survey—especially when contrasted with the previous one—makes it clear that if you have the choice, you should definitely take the "tough" that you find at the top. "On average," noted *The Economist,* "Oscar winners live about four years more than other Hollywood actors, and at either end of a 12-mile subway ride between poor downtown Washington, D.C., and rich white Montgomery County, there is a difference in life expectancy of 20 years."[8]

We will return to the fact that life is tough, both at the top and at the bottom, in subsequent chapters—and talk about what CEOs need to do to make it easier.

3

DEREGULATION, CONCENTRATION, AND WORM JUICE

The more things change, the more they stay the same.

Or, in the context of deregulation and the industry concentration that tends to follow it, it's more like, *The worse things get, the more likely they are to wind up where they started, only worse.*

The deregulatory push, when it began back in the 1970s, had good intentions. After all, deregulation started under Jimmy Carter, whom most people (even his detractors) would call the embodiment of good intentions. But deregulation then drifted into the zone of unintended consequences. It wound up wreaking havoc in the transportation, telecom, and utility industries. Once-proud companies failed or were acquired, and concentration ensued. And when that happened, corporations misbehaved, and consumers got screwed.

What happens when consumers get screwed? Two things. First, consumers—hard to arouse, but also hard to calm down—stand up and defend their interests. And a couple of steps behind them come the politicians, eager to jump on the bandwagon, identify and vilify the "bad guys," and pass laws that reallocate the power. This reallocation is often counterproductive. It is sometimes motivated by political agendas that actually have zero to do with helping the consumer but are nonetheless wrapped in that garb.

Take free speech: toward the end of this chapter, I'll look once again at the industry that I know best—the cable/broadcast/entertainment industry—and make the case that the deregulation and concentration that have occurred there have sown the seeds for, among other things, an assault on free speech. No, we can't and shouldn't turn back the clock. In fact, there is no "golden age" of regulation that we can go back to. Almost by definition, regulation breeds inefficiencies and therefore can be a drag on the economy. But we *can* steer toward a better future. It will take a CEO, or, in this case, several of them, to impose the kind of self-restraint that the media industry must embrace.

THE BEST INTENTIONS

In the late 1970s, the federal government launched a process of deregulating key industries, beginning with the airlines. The Airline Deregulation Act of 1978, championed by Alfred Kahn and others, was the first major result of this larger effort.

The theory was that government controls that dated back to the early days of the Civil Aeronautics Board (CAB) had created an unnatural constraint on competition in the domestic commercial airline industry. Lift the heavy hand of government control—so the advocates of deregulation argued—and a new era of competition and innovation would begin. Ticket prices would fall dramatically. Airline passengers would enjoy far greater choices. The magic of the market would allow a hundred flowers to bloom.

It didn't work out quite that way.

Why? Well, first of all, the logic of airline deregulation was fundamentally flawed. Alfred Kahn and his supporters made their case based largely on a single example, between an unregulated instate California airline carrying passengers between San Francisco and Los Angeles (a high-volume, no-frills route) and the average fares of regulated airlines flying routes between states. Guess which looked better.[1]

So what happened in the wake of deregulation? A large number of established carriers seized upon the opportunity of deregulation to pursue strategies that the CAB had traditionally blocked. The problem was that in a deregulated world, these were dumb strategies. In the "bad old days" of regulation, the CAB allocated market share on certain routes to specific carriers, a system that protected profitability. This arrangement argued for lots of high-traffic, point-to-point routes, fed by "feeder systems" from smaller airports. When regulation went away, the smart airlines shifted to hub systems, inducements like frequent-flyer programs, and domination of the channels where travelers purchased tickets.

Braniff, Western, Eastern, and Pan American didn't get it. Rather than setting up fortresslike hubs—where they could dominate the market and throw their weight around—they focused heavily on long-distance routes and got their lunches eaten by low-cost upstarts. Have you tried to buy a ticket on one of those four airlines recently? Or, for that matter, on Allegheny, Southern, Ozark, Piedmont, or TransTexas? Don't bother; they're history.[2]

So you had a bunch of brash new entrants coming into the industry, cherry-picking among the most profitable routes and taking no responsibility for setting up or maintaining expensive feeder systems. Meanwhile, they are paying their employees much less than the established airlines and otherwise fueling yet another downward spiral. Not surprisingly, revenue per mile per seat has fallen 4.5 percent annually (on average) since 1978.[3] The established carriers, hemorrhaging money, are demanding more and more concessions from their unionized workforces.

Yes, airfares fell by something like 40 percent in the two decades following deregulation, and that's a good thing—if, that is, you can find a flight that's going where you want to go (and there's a seat, and you don't mind a connection or two, and you don't expect to get food on board, and you don't want a paper ticket, and you don't mind talking with a ticket agent in Bangalore, and so on). But guess what? That decline in airfares—40 percent—is almost exactly as much as airfares fell in the two decades *preceding* deregulation, according to *Consumer Reports*.[4]

The airline industry is becoming more like the bus industry: unprofitable, cheap, crowded, and stripped of all creature comforts. People are flying more and enjoying it less.

So deregulation hasn't lived up to its advance billing, in terms of either better service or lower fares. Many smaller U.S. cities have experienced drastic cutbacks in airline service. You could make the case, moreover, that at least some of the reduced prices in the post-deregulation era have been subsidized by the $10 billion pot (of taxpayer money) that Congress put together to keep the airlines afloat in the wake of 9/11. And if you travel on business, which often means traveling on short notice, you're probably not getting any bargains; in fact, you're probably getting soaked by your monopolistic hub-based carrier. As Robert Kuttner recently wrote, in an article in *Prospect* on the on-again, off-again bankruptcy of US Airways,

> What's truly amazing is that US Airways could go bankrupt, despite tactics that would make an old-fashioned robber-baron monopolist blush. For instance, US Airways has a monopoly on nonstops between Washington and Boston. It charges around $670 for a basic roundtrip fare. It controls 74 percent of flights in and out of Philadelphia, and charges as much as $550 for a roundtrip flight between Pittsburgh and Harrisburg, Pa. It is literally cheaper, and almost as fast, to take a taxi.[5]

But there's another, more fundamental problem here. Industries that are high-stakes activities with significant public-policy implications have to be held to a different standard. There is a public trust involved. Taking hundreds of people 30,000 feet up into the sky and shooting through the air at 500 miles per hour, in a vehicle that can be turned into a weapon of devastating power or can be brought down by bad maintenance or a tired pilot, is not the same thing as making widgets.

That was the logic behind regulation in the first place, and to a large extent, it was the right logic. The meatpackers and patent-medicine manufacturers howled, way back in 1906, when Congress passed the Pure Food and Drug Act, which did nothing more than require manufacturers to reveal what was in their products. Decades later, the automakers howled when the government mandated padded dashboards, seat belts, headrests, air-pollution-control devices, airbags, and so on. Businesses with established ways of doing things don't like the government intruding. Well, tough luck. The foods we ingest and the air we breathe are rightly subject to regulation.

So is the air we fly in. Pre-9/11, airport security was essentially left to the airlines—those same airlines whose profit margins had been squeezed out of existence by the cherry-picking upstarts. So when it came to the boring and unprofitable job of security, the airlines raced to the bottom, which meant that airport checkpoint jobs became low-wage, high-turnover positions. (What did people *think* was going to happen, under those circumstances?) Then came the tragedy of 9/11, and the government created the Transportation Safety Administration and took over airport security.

Let me underscore this point. The deregulation of the airline industry ultimately led to a massive government intervention in that industry, with 40,000 more people on the government payroll.

The Canadians—sometimes vulnerable to bad influences by their neighbor to the south—deregulated their airlines in 1987, with very similar results to those in the United States: chaos and concentration. By 1993, two airlines dominated Canada, and they were locked in a cutthroat competition that threatened the viability of both. A howl went up, and the reregulation debate began.

Here's the prescription contained in a minority report to the Canadian Parliament:

> Modern regulation means taking a flexible approach and using government powers selectively to ensure that airlines compete fairly and live up to their public trust. Profitable high-traffic routes, like Toronto-Montreal-Ottawa, will naturally attract competition among carriers. These routes do not need government regulation to ensure adequate service. The role the government needs to play is that of a referee, to ensure fair competition and prevent damaging anti-competitive behavior such as predatory pricing and excessive capacity.
>
> On the other hand, low-traffic routes between smaller communities are not guaranteed to attract service. In these cases, effective regulation is essential, because reasonable and affordable service is a social and economic necessity. The government has

many tools at its disposal to ensure service to such communities, including incentives, tendering, and cross-subsidy. The Canadian government is far from impotent; many creative options are available to ensure long-term service to such communities.[6]

That is straight talk from the north, and it bears on our own circumstances. Our government too is "far from impotent." But recent history suggests that it may not assert itself at the right time, or in the right way.

CALIFORNIA AND ENRON

After the airlines, one of the next major industries to be subject to deregulation was the electric utility industry. The deregulation of wholesale electricity prices actually started in Britain in the 1970s and was imported into the States—basically on a state-by-state basis—beginning in the 1990s.

Again, the theory was that the utility industry had been coddled unnaturally by government. By allowing the same companies to control generation, transmission, and distribution—the deregulators argued—and by establishing local monopolies and fixed rates, the government was artificially inflating electricity prices and hurting consumers. Once again, as the argument went, if the heavy hand of government were lifted, the resulting competition would drive prices down for consumers.

The argument was wrong. Like flying people through the sky, electricity isn't widgets. The demand for electricity is relatively inelastic. (This is the economist's way of saying that while you're likely to forgo buying an overpriced Pepsi, you're going to keep buying electricity almost no matter what it costs.) Supply too is inelastic: building a new generating plant is incredibly expensive and time-consuming—it takes up to a decade—and very often controversial. The normal economic checks and balances don't apply. And if you can't get competition at the wholesale level, you won't get lower prices to the consumer.

California led the way in utility deregulation in the United States, with the passage of legislation in 1996 allowing consumers to choose their electricity provider. It's fair to say that the experiment didn't go well. The nation watched in disbelief, during the summer of 2001, as California writhed and struggled with seemingly inadequate power supplies and ultimately was compelled to enter into extortionate long-term contracts just to keep the lights on. Prices quadrupled at the consumer level. In September of that year, the California Public Utilities Commission effectively abandoned its foray into deregulation.

What was not so clear at the time was the role of Enron, the now much-disgraced and bankrupt corporate villain, in this fiasco. Unfortunately for California's consumers, the federal government made two missteps that almost guaranteed that California would take a hit. In 1994, Enron got the Securities and Exchange Commission to agree that it shouldn't be subject to the rules that applied to multistate utility companies. (The rationale was that Enron didn't *generate* power; it only *marketed* power.) Then, in 2000—with a strong push from Texas senator Phil Gramm, who certainly didn't mind doing Houston-based Enron a big favor—Congress deregulated the trading of energy futures. Now Enron could pursue its schemes without fear of scrutiny from either the SEC or the stock exchanges.

And scheme it did. Starting in approximately May 2000 and continuing into the following year, Enron engaged in a number of illegal practices—collectively called "gaming"—designed to evade energy price caps under the pretense of importing electricity into the western states. It formed stealth partnerships to control power resources, create artificial shortages, and manipulate prices upward. By overcharging customers, Enron was succeeding in skimming off up to $2 million *a day* from California, as well as additional sums from electricity consumers in other neighboring states in the tightly connected western grid.

Belatedly, the Department of Justice and FBI launched criminal probes of Enron's western electricity traders. These probes turned up tape recordings of phone calls among those traders. Following is an excerpt from an actual conversation between two individuals identified as Bob Badeer and Kevin McGowan, on November 30, 2000. Fair warning—the language gets a little rough:

Kevin: So the rumor's true? They're fuckin' takin' all the money back from you guys? All those money you guys stole from those poor grandmothers in California?

Bob: Yeah, Grandma Millie, man. But she's the one who couldn't figure out how to fuckin' vote on the butterfly ballot.

Kevin: Yeah, now she wants her fuckin' money back for all the power you've charged right up—jammed right up her ass for fuckin' 250 dollars a megawatt hour.

[*laughter*]

Bob: You know—you know—you know, Grandma Millie, she's the one that Al Gore's fightin' for, you know.

A little later in the same conversation, Kevin laughingly tells Bob about a consultant to Enron who happened to live in California and who on the previous day had visited the Enron facility where Kevin worked:

Kevin: He was talking to George McClellan and George's desk, and he's like, "Yeah, you know, I'm in California now and my small consulting business, my energy costs have gone from 100 to 500 dollars a month. It's unbelievable, I don't know what to do." I just turned from my desk, I just looked at him, I said, "MOVE."

[*laughter*]

Kevin: The guy was horrified. I go, "Look, don't take it the wrong way. Move; it isn't getting fixed any time soon."[7]

Federal regulators imposed price controls on the California energy market in June 2001. As late as October of that year, according to *The Washington Post,* Enron CEO Kenneth Lay had the audacity to get up in front of a group of policy makers in Washington and assert that "with more energy deregulation, Enron and the nation [would] continue to flourish."[8]

Enron collapsed two months later. The collapse meant the taking-down of the retirement packages of thousands of hapless and blameless Enron workers, and it did great damage to the Houston economy. We will return to Enron, and similar corporate rogues, in subsequent chapters. But I bring up the case here because it's such an over-the-top example of the dark side of deregulation and excessive industry concentration. Yes, prior to deregulation, many utilities were fat, dumb, and happy. And yes, sometimes they gouged consumers, in a penny-ante way—maybe a few extra cents on your residential rate. But they did so in the context of a game whose rules were clearly specified. By and large, they accepted the idea that there was a public trust inherent in their work. They didn't sit around and talk about sticking it to Grandma Millie.

The New England Electric System (NEES) was a regional utility that was broken up in the 1990s when Massachusetts (following California's lead) deregulated its utilities. With the end in sight, the company published a corporate history celebrating more than a century of service to New England. Then-president and CEO of NEES, John W. Rowe, wrote an eloquent foreword to the book, which included the following passage:

> Competition, for all its virtues, also threatens deeper values. In my mind, NEES and other high-performing utilities are great middle-class institutions. They are full of people who want to do good for their communities, while earning a decent and stable living. I've long said that if your car were to break down and you had to leave your baby somewhere while you went to get help, the best place to leave that baby would be a lineman's truck. Those two or three burly guys would take such good care of that child![9]

Well said. And because the utilities were on the hook—they were the clearly responsible party, if something went wrong—they took responsibility for keeping the grid in reasonable health. When the widespread blackout of August 2003 occurred throughout the Midwest and East, most people could agree on only one thing: the transmission network had been neglected. Think about it: postregulation, nobody had a particularly strong stake in keeping the transmission and distribution capabilities up to snuff. And by the way, if you're going to foster competition on the grid, you need a bigger, stronger grid on which to stage that competition. A weak grid necessarily means weak competition.

Here's an irony: in the wake of the blackout, the Federal Energy Regulatory Commission (FERC) proposed (in late 2003) to expand its oversight of the transmission system.[10] This proposal met with a chilly reception from the White House and from Senate Republicans. And a year later, when FERC issued its final report on the blackout, it continued to make careful, plaintive noises about the need to reregulate. "Many U.S. parties that should be required by law to comply with reliability requirements," wrote FERC, "are not subject to the Commission's full authorities under the Federal Power Act."[11]

So far, reregulation hasn't happened—an amazing fact, in light of the Great Western Power Rip-off of 2000–2001 (as orchestrated by Enron) and the 2003 blackout. What's it going to take for consumers to say, "Enough's enough!"

And what kind of reregulation will we see, at that point?

MEDIA DEREGULATION AND CONCENTRATION: A TWO-HEADED MONSTER

Let's look at a third industry—media—for another example of the perils of precipitous deregulation.

For many years, the Federal Communications Commission (FCC) operated on the theory that media concentration was a bad thing. In other words, you shouldn't let one person or company own all the newspapers, television stations, or radio stations in one town. Equally, you shouldn't let one person or company own too many media outlets across the nation. Both kinds of media concentration were seen as being bad for democracy.

Beginning in the mid-1980s, however, the FCC—under the influence of both deregulation advocates and the probusiness Reagan administration—changed the rules to make it easier for media moguls to own multiple TV stations. This trend continued into the new century, to the extent that by the beginning of 2003, the FCC was issuing new regulations permitting a single company to own multiple outlets in the same market. In June 2003, the Senate Commerce Committee weighed in against the move, with both Republican and Democratic senators voting to overturn the FCC's rule changes. A federal appeals court also blocked the FCC from moving in this direction.

So what happened next? According to the *New York Times*, the FCC went ahead and relaxed the rules informally, thereby making a "mockery" of media concentration rules.[12] Apparently the FCC is quite comfortable with the example of Clear Channel Communications—which controlled 40 radio stations in 1996 and today controls more than 1,200 nationwide—and doesn't mind the prospect of similar consolidations in other media.[13]

Media deregulation and concentration are a two-headed monster. What are the two heads? First, media concentration remains a threat to our democratic processes. You don't want one person or company telling an entire media market how to think. You want competition in the realm of ideas. This was the line of reasoning that was followed by both the Senate Commerce Committee and the federal appeals court, in the sequence described above.

I'll return to this topic at length in the next chapter. Meanwhile, let me talk briefly about the other head of the monster: the race to the bottom. The major media companies today think that they can get away with acting like Afghani warlords. Wielders of immense power, and not much concerned about a regulatory community that they see as largely ineffectual, they feel free to chase ratings in any way they see fit. At the same time, because they have an enemy to their left and another to their right, they feel compelled to chase those ratings.

One result is Janet Jackson's right breast popping up in prime time.

Another result is a truly sleazy made-for-TV movie, *Call Me: The Rise and Fall of Heidi Fleiss,* which aired on the USA Network in March 2004, a few months after the notorious Super Bowl halftime show. This television movie, according to *New York Post* columnist Adam Buckman, was "as close as basic cable has ever come to pornography."[14]

Another result is *The Swan,* a truly loathsome show produced by the Fox Network. As you may not know if you've been lucky enough to avoid this one, the show subjects two self-defined "ugly-duckling" women to every sort of physical makeover, up to and including plastic surgery. Then one gets picked, and one gets sent packing. Here's one reviewer's take:

> When TV gets this ugly, duck. Hurtful and repellent even by reality's constantly plummeting standards, *The Swan* is proof that the genre's hucksters have no built-in boundaries. They will plumb ever-lower depths until the market, or the courts, stop them. For anyone wondering where to draw the line, here it is: Janet Jackson's breast reveal was tasteless, *The Swan* is obscene.[15]

Another result is *Fear Factor*. This slimy bit of programming—remarkable both for its complete lack of decency and its longevity—premiered in June 2000; it has found a large audience ever since. NBC used *Fear Factor* to plug a hole in its Monday night lineup, apparently not expecting much. Since then, the show has turned into one of the biggest hits on TV. This success, in turn, has allowed its producers to gradually raise the stakes. In year one, contestants only had to do things like eat eyeballs. By year three, they were Dumpster diving.[16]

Want to read a truly disgusting, depressing, demoralizing article? Try the story on the front page of the *Wall Street Journal*'s April 29, 2004, edition, which describes the difficulties that the producers of *Fear Factor* have in keeping the show "fresh":

> As [*Fear Factor* executive producer Matt] Kunitz says, "There are only so many things you can do with a worm." To date, contestants have had to eat worms, sit in a coffin filled with worms, bury their head in worms and shower with syrup-covered worms. What about having people stamp on thousands of night crawlers with their feet and then drink the resulting brown paste from a crystal goblet? It's been done.[17]

It may have been done, but it *shouldn't* have been done. Similarly in the sexual realm: the fact that you can get away with something doesn't mean it's right. According to a recent study by the American Academy of Pediatrics, 56 percent of all programs on American television contained sexual content, the average "family hour" (8:00–9:00 p.m.) contains more than eight sexual incidents, and a sample fifty hours of soap operas included 156 acts of sexual intercourse, with only five mentions of safe sex or contraception.[18]

Can this sort of thing go on, and get worse, indefinitely? No. The worse things get, the more likely they are to wind up where they started, only worse.

THE TRAP OF CONCENTRATION

In 2003, Morgan Stanley issued a report on the U.S. airline industry. "If an industry produces negative total returns on capital over its entire history," the investment banking firm asserted, "consolidation is inevitable."[19]

Yes, this is the voice of untrammeled capitalism speaking— *If they've got too many seats, let the dinosaurs die!*—but the conclusion is sound. If an industry goes into a tailspin due to deregulation-induced chaos (in addition to bad management and externalities like high fuel prices and terrorist attacks), industry concentration is inevitable.

The problem is, consolidation leads almost inevitably to some sort of abuse, which leads in turn to government intervention. We deregulate to get government out of the way and to let the free market do what the free market does best. Then the deregulated industry goes into convulsions, the strong eat the weak, and we wind up with a monopolistic/oligopolistic structure in which the consumers' needs aren't being met (whether in terms of cost, safety, good taste, or some other measure). Or in which an Enron gleefully sticks it to Grandma Millie (and millions of other consumers). A cry goes up, the politicians respond, and the government goes back into the offending industry. The worse things get, the more likely they are to wind up back where they started, only worse.

In the late 1990s and early 2000s, you didn't often find Congressman Tom DeLay and Senator Tom Daschle agreeing on things. But both the überconservative Republican congressman from Texas and the progressive Democratic senator from South Dakota backed an increase in the fines levied on broadcasters for violating indecency rules. Interestingly, Daschle has found a direct link between the rise in media concentration and the rise in objectionable content.[20]

It's more than a little ironic that the misdeeds of the ultimate poster child of untrammeled capitalism—Enron—led more or less directly to the passage of Sarbanes-Oxley. Why ironic? Because this is the law that requires CEOs to sign on the bottom line, attesting to the veracity of their financial reports, on pain of jail terms. Talk about trammels! All of a sudden, we are starting to hear executives singing the praises of "going private"—that is, of taking a publicly held corporation private—in order to avoid having to follow the rules of "fair disclosure" and sign on the bottom line. The worse things get, the more likely they are to wind up back where they started, only worse.

GETTING OUT OF WAUSAU

Sometimes you hear a story on the news, and it brings you up short. Selfishly, you first count your own blessings: you say, "Jeez, I'm glad I'm not in *that* poor guy's shoes!" And sometimes, if you reflect on the issue a little more, you go on to say, "There but for the grace of God go I."

That was my experience a few months back, when National Public Radio broadcast a longish report on Greyhound Line's plans to end bus service to a number of cities and small towns in the Midwest, starting in August 2004. One of those cities was Wausau, Wisconsin.

Dallas-based Greyhound lost $112 million in 2002. It reduced that figure to $29 million the following year—obviously, a big step in the right direction, from the point of view of the shareholders of Laidlaw International, Greyhound's parent company. The cuts announced in the summer of 2004 were intended to help keep the company moving toward the black. Of course, the fact that Greyhound was in the black before the turn-of-the-twenty-first-century recession set in does raise the question as to whether it was necessary to cut service to 260 communities in thirteen states in the Upper Midwest and Northwest, but fortunately, I'm not in the bus-strategy business.

Moreover, I know nothing at all about Wausau, Wisconsin, which turns out to be only one of 47 Wisconsin cities scheduled to lose their bus service. And I have no idea what it means to the residents, or the economy, of Wisconsin that you can no longer get from Green Bay to Eau Claire because the connection through Wausau has been dropped.[21] But a local newspaper account about a resident of the small town of Gleason gives a taste of what must be happening in and around Wausau. The story concerns an eighty-year-old woman named Marion Forecki, who rode the bus six times a year to Wausau to visit family members there.

"I don't know how I'm going to get around," she told a *Wausau Daily Herald* reporter. "It's ridiculous. They want to have old people retested again [for driver's licenses]. How are we supposed to get around?"[22]

Good question. What happened to Marion Forecki? Basically, deregulators decided way back in 1982 that she and people like her weren't important. The Bus Regulatory Reform Act deregulated intercity bus services in that year, and bus service has been declining ever since. Yes, people love their cars more every year, and that hurts the bus trade. But at least to some extent, this is a circular problem: people *have* to love their cars more if every other means of transport is either crappy or nonexistent. (Let's watch to see if car registrations by seniors in Wausau rise in the coming years.) There was a researcher at the Federal Communications Commission who in 2004 produced an industry-by-industry survey of regulation in the United States. In the study, he relegated buses to a footnote. "Scheduled intercity bus service . . . was a small and declining industry that has been little studied," he wrote. "I follow the common practice of simply ignoring it."[23]

Yep. The question is, do we like where deregulation has taken us? Is it OK if the economic life of 260 communities is disrupted, 150 Greyhound workers are laid off, and the Marion Foreckis of the world can't get in or out of Wausau, all because a corporation says that's the way it has to be?

Is it enough to say, "Jeez, I'm glad I'm not in *that* poor guy's (or woman's) shoes"?

ONCE AGAIN, IT TAKES A CEO

These are not easy topics. There are no simple solutions.

Maybe the declining ridership of scheduled intercity buses won't rise up in revolt. (They're too old, too poor, and too disorganized.) Maybe the beleaguered airline passengers will continue to take what's dished out to them. I note with interest that the Central Wisconsin Airport (CWA), which serves Wausau, had a banner year in 2003: a record 305,291 passengers. At the same time, according to the *Wausau Daily Herald,* the board that runs that airport is considering applying for a federal grant aimed at helping small airports that are underserved or facing higher-than-average ticket costs. Reading between the lines, deregulation has proved to be a double-edged sword for CWA.[24]

And what happens if, tomorrow, Northwest Airlines decides to eliminate service to CWA? It could happen: in June 2004, Standard & Poor's downgraded Northwest's debt rating, and the airline continues to struggle with a relatively high cost structure.

When it comes to industries that are high-stakes and involve a public trust, *all of us have a role to play.* In industries where competition is impossible (for example, the utility business), government has a role to play. Equally, in industries where our lives or our moral fiber is at stake (airlines and the media, respectively), government must play a role.

At the same time, we consumers are going to have to speak up for ourselves. If you don't like what's getting served up to you, or if you think you're being gouged, *raise the roof.*

And finally, the leadership of the private sector—CEOs and other senior leaders—is simply going to have to come to grips with these issues. First of all, it's the *practical* thing to do. (If we don't do it, the government will.) Second, and more important, it's also the *right* thing to do.

4

PUTTING DEMOCRACY ON
THE BLOCK

The deregulation of the media industry, as noted in the previous chapter, has proven a two-headed monster. The two heads are 1) a race to the bottom, as evidenced by shows like *Fear Factor,* and 2) a threat to democracy. We've already looked at the first of these issues. Now let's dig deeper into the second and more serious issue: the threat to our democracy that is posed by the casual and cavalier deregulation by the FCC of one of the most important industries in the nation.

Maybe you're thinking that these alarm bells are being sounded by a former media CEO with an ax to grind. Maybe you're thinking that, yes, electricity and air travel are necessities and economic spark plugs and therefore can be described as repositories of the public trust, but the *media*? Are we exaggerating to make a point here?

Well, as somebody once commented, journalism is the only profession with its own constitutional amendment. There were compelling reasons to pass that amendment, and those reasons still pertain today. I'm betting that you won't get through our next case history—about the practices of a company called the Sinclair Broadcast Group—without at least starting to share my sense of great disquiet: we're on a very dangerous path, and we're moving way too quickly down that path.

Through reckless deregulation of the media industry, and through the vertical and horizontal integration that has resulted, we're putting our democracy on the block.

SAYING NO TO *NIGHTLINE*

On Tuesday, April 27, 2004, ABC News announced that it had prepared a special edition of *Nightline,* scheduled to air at 11:35 p.m. on April 30. The special, entitled *The Fallen,* would consist of host Ted Koppel's reading the names of all the U.S. troops killed in Iraq up to that point—a roster that then included 523 men and women—while their photographs rolled by on the screen.

The conservative talk-show crowd didn't quite know what to make of this. Several days before the show's broadcast, Rush Limbaugh told his radio audience that the *Nightline* special wasn't necessarily a *bad* idea, but he huffed a bit about how maybe ABC would capitalize on *The Fallen* to boost ratings during the May sweeps (which included April 30). Fox's prominent conservative Bill O'Reilly decided not to criticize a show that he hadn't yet seen. On the other hand, he did express his conditional disapproval of the broadcast, commenting that "to exploit the suffering of military people defending their country undermines morale."[1]

Not suffering from any lack of clarity that week was the Hunt Valley, Maryland–based Sinclair Broadcast Group. On Thursday, April 29, Sinclair instructed its seven ABC affiliates not to air *The Fallen.* According to an online statement issued by Sinclair,

> Despite the denials by a spokeswoman for the show, the action appears to be motivated by a political agenda designed to undermine the efforts of the United States in Iraq.
>
> There is no organization that holds the members of our military and those soldiers who have sacrificed their lives in service of our country in higher regard than Sinclair Broadcast Group. While Sinclair would support an honest effort to honor the memory of these brave soldiers, we do not believe that is what "Night-

line" is doing. Rather, Mr. Koppel and "Nightline" are hiding behind this so-called tribute in an effort to highlight only one aspect of the war effort and in doing so to influence public opinion against the military action in Iraq. Based on published reports, we are aware of the spouse of one soldier who died in Iraq who opposes the reading of her husband's name to oppose our military action. We suspect she is not alone in this viewpoint. As a result, we have decided to preempt the broadcast of "Nightline" this Friday on each of our stations which air ABC programming.

We understand that our decision in this matter may be questioned by some. Before you judge our decision, however, we would ask that you first question Mr. Koppel as to why he chose to read the names of 523 troops killed in combat in Iraq, rather than the names of the thousands of private citizens killed in terrorist attacks since and including the events of September 11, 2001. In his answer, we believe you will find the real motivation behind his action scheduled for this Friday. Unfortunately, we may never know for sure because Mr. Koppel has refused repeated requests from Sinclair's News Central news organization to comment on this Friday's program.[2]

All in all, a nasty little piece of writing. The moguls at Sinclair ignored denials from *Nightline* that the show was intended to "undermine" the U.S. military. They quoted an unnamed widow who opposed "the reading of her husband's name to oppose our military action"—as, presumably, *most* family members of slain service people would, if the question were put to them in just that way. Sinclair hit upon a sneaky way to link Iraq with September 11—a link that has never been substantiated. Finally, the company criticized Koppel for not returning their calls to explain himself to them.

Who is this Sinclair Broadcast Group, and where does it get off scolding Ted Koppel?

According to its Web site, the company began as a single UHF station in Baltimore in 1971, under the guidance of founder Julian Sinclair Smith. His four sons eventually purchased the company from him and set out to transform it into what they now call (on their corporate Web site) a "major consolidator" in the broadcasting industry. One way they did so was to use what's known as local marketing agreements, or LMAs, to get around FCC rules prohibiting ownership of more than one station in a local market.[3] Simply put, Sinclair would buy one local station and then buy the assets—but not the license—of another local station, a dodge that was permissible under FCC guidelines. By 1996, Sinclair was, in its own words, the "nation's largest commercial television company not owned by a network."[4] Sinclair also built a strong radio presence alongside its television empire, but it eventually sold off its fifty-five radio stations to concentrate on TV.

Today, the company owns or provides programming to more than sixty stations across the country, reaching close to 25 percent of all U.S. households. In addition to its seven ABC affiliates, the group includes twenty Fox stations, nineteen WB affiliates, six UPN outlets, three CBS affiliates, and four NBC affiliates.[5]

One of Julian Sinclair Smith's four sons, David D. Smith, serves as the company's chairman, president, and CEO. Along with his three brothers, Smith controls about 95 percent of the company (which went public in June 1995).[6] According to the *Wall Street Journal* and other public records, the Smiths are very significant contributors to the Republican National Committee and to individual Republican candidates.[7]

Well, fine. They can support whomever they want to support. But let's dig a little deeper into how the Sinclair empire's political agenda insinuates itself into the American political discourse. The chances are one in four that you are being exposed to this agenda. If so, you're getting it on a daily basis, and in ways that you may not realize.

In the press release quoted above, did you catch the reference to "Sinclair's News Central news organization"? This is a good example of the proverbial wolf in sheep's clothing. Beginning in 2002, Sinclair started experimenting with a system of offering packaged news in smaller markets that allegedly couldn't provide a broad-enough range of products to their viewers. The result is a hybrid of local content interspersed with material from Sinclair's Baltimore-based central news operation, called News Central. On the screen, you see (for example) the Raleigh anchor engaged in lighthearted dialogue with the meteorologist about the weather outside, but un-beknownst to the viewer, that meteorologist talking about conditions in Raleigh happens to be in faraway Baltimore. Meanwhile, studio wizards seamlessly blend together this dubious "local" content with prepackaged material that goes out to all of the News Central stations.

The first five cities in which this concept was tested were Minneapolis, Flint, Oklahoma City, Raleigh, and Rochester—not exactly underresourced media markets. The concept has expanded rapidly. According to Sinclair's Web site, there are now thirty-eight stations around the country participating in News Central. In seven markets (Baltimore, Champagne-Springfield-Decatur, Charleston-Huntington, Columbus, Dayton, Greensboro, and Las Vegas), there are *two* Sinclair stations engaging in simulated local news.[8]

One prepackaged feature that goes to *all* the News Central stations is a noxious little segment called "The Point." It features a loudmouth named Mark Hyman, who objects to whatever allegedly left-leaning thing is annoying him at the moment.

The problem is that Mark Hyman is neither a pundit nor a reporter, nor is he particularly qualified to tell the citizens of Madison *anything*. In real life, he is Sinclair's vice president of corporate communications. So it was Mark Hyman that the *Wall Street Journal* called during that last week of April 2004, seeking clarification of his company's decision to preempt *Nightline*. "He didn't return calls seeking comment," the *Journal* reported.

What happened next? Arizona Senator John McCain—who has, over the years, earned the respect of people across the broad political spectrum—fired off a letter to Sinclair's David Smith:

> I write to strongly protest your decision to instruct Sinclair's ABC affiliates to preempt this evening's *Nightline* program. I find deeply offensive Sinclair's objection to *Nightline*'s intention to broadcast the names and photographs of Americans who gave their lives in service to our country in Iraq.
>
> I supported the President's decision to go to war to Iraq, and remain a strong supporter of that decision. But every American has a responsibility to understand fully the terrible costs of war

and the extraordinary sacrifices it requires of those brave men and women who volunteer to defend the rest of us; lest we ever forget or grow insensitive to how grave a decision it is for our government to order Americans into combat. It is a solemn responsibility of elected officials to accept responsibility for our decision and its consequences, and, with those who disseminate the news, to ensure that Americans are fully informed of those consequences.

There is no valid reason for Sinclair to shirk its responsibility in what I assume is a very misguided attempt to prevent your viewers from completely appreciating the extraordinary sacrifices made on their behalf by Americans serving in Iraq. War is an awful, but sometimes necessary business. Your decision to deny your viewers an opportunity to be reminded of war's terrible costs, in all their heartbreaking detail, is a gross disservice to the public, and to the men and women of the United States Armed Forces. It is, in short, sir, unpatriotic. I hope it meets with the public opprobrium it most certainly deserves.[9]

Of course, as a broadcaster, you don't want to have a figure like John McCain calling you "unpatriotic" if you can possibly avoid it. But the larger points come in McCain's second paragraph. Elected officials have to be held accountable for their decisions. Those who disseminate the news have a solemn responsibility to make sure Americans are *fully informed* of the consequences of decisions made by those elected officials. (That's why we licensed the airwaves to them in the first place.) In other words, when you shoulder the responsibilities of a broadcaster, you don't get a menu: you're not entitled to take a little from here and a little from there—depending on your political agenda—and serve up the result to the viewing public.

The good news, in this unhappy tale, is that the viewing public objected strenuously to Sinclair's high-handed actions. "I have not gotten one positive response," said the assignment desk editor at Sinclair's Columbus, Ohio, affiliate, who gets credit for courage.[10] The other good news—at least for the time being—is that the Sinclair Broadcast Group is not yet a truly major player in the industry. (Surprised that owning or controlling sixty TV stations, and reaching a quarter of the country, doesn't make you a big player? Read on.)

But the bad news is that Sinclair is already *acting* like one of the big boys. What do I mean by that? The bigger a media company becomes, the more political it becomes, and the more insulated it becomes from viewer expressions of anger about incomplete or imbalanced reporting. The easier it becomes for the people in charge of that company to sway its programming, at the expense of the public trust that's been invested in them.

So even before becoming one of the big boys, Sinclair is misbehaving like one of them.

THE DEATH OF DIVERSITY

Consolidation and homogenization of the media product are very, very dangerous. It means that a much smaller, and much less diverse, collection of viewpoints gets heard.

Let's be clear: I don't blame companies like Sinclair for consolidating to achieve economies of scale. Nor do I blame them for favoring national or syndicated programming over local programming. (The former is much cheaper than the latter.) "You can't repeal the laws of economics," as the saying goes. Corporations will, and *should,* pursue their economic interests within the limits of the law.

That means, of course, that we have to make sure that our laws—and associated regulations—put appropriate constraints on media enterprises. Over the past two decades, the FCC has made a series of mistaken rulings that have served to weaken or remove those vital constraints. It's time to turn the train around.

What's the history? In the first few decades after World War II, Congress and the FCC took steps to ensure that *more* voices would be heard. It required TV manufacturers to build sets that could receive both VHF and UHF signals, thereby creating a market for UHF television. It limited to seven the number of stations a single company could own. It set aside a large number of UHF stations for independent owners.[11] *Let a hundred flowers bloom* seemed to be the dominant philosophy among the regulators, *and regulate in such a way as to promote those blooms.*

Then came Jimmy Carter's deregulation, and thereafter came the strongly probusiness Reagan administration. In 1984, the FCC raised the cap on station ownership by a single entity from seven to twelve. Although it imposed an "audience cap" (the size of the overall national audience a single entity could reach) in 1985, it raised that cap (from 25 percent to 35 percent) in 1996—the same year that it completely did away with caps on the total number of stations a business could own. In 2003, as we've seen, the FCC tried to get rid of most of the remaining restrictions on ownership of media outlets, only to be overruled by Congress and the courts.

But there's another, more insidious kind of consolidation that has been happening over the course of this history: the combination within a single media company of both the production and the distribution of content. In 1970, the FCC became concerned about the growing power of the three networks (CBS, NBC, and ABC) to control programming. Between 1957 and 1968, the FCC pointed out, the percentage of network shows produced by independent production companies dropped from 33 percent to 4 percent. The agency therefore passed the Financial Interest and Syndication Rules, informally known as Fin-Syn, designed to protect independent production companies. By preventing networks from reselling programs that they had already aired, Fin-Syn compelled the networks to sell off their syndication arms. Once again, the philosophy was *Let a hundred flowers bloom.*

But in the early 1990s, the networks began making the case that Fin-Syn was outdated and irrelevant. When the FCC bought this logic, the networks began buying up the independent production companies. It didn't take long. "In 1985," commented Consumers Union media watchdog Gene Kimmelman in testimony before Congress, "there were 25 independent television production studios. . . . In 2002, however, only 5 independent television studios remained." And whereas in 1992, only 15 percent of new TV shows were produced by a network-controlled studio, by 2002, that number had increased to 77 percent.)[12]

Here's an irony: as the networks became more profitable, they became more attractive as acquisition targets themselves. One by one, they were swallowed up by big corporations: GE (NBC), Cap Cities (ABC, later acquired by Disney), and Viacom (CBS). Picture those fish lined up from smaller to larger, each getting eaten by somebody bigger.

Increasingly, the point became to own *everything*—to your left and to your right, and both up and down the production chain. The FCC went along with this consolidation at every turn. Ted Turner (who unabashedly admits to having participated in this game to the hilt, back when he controlled his TNT/CNN/MGM empire) now looks at the result of all this consolidation with great concern:

> Today, the only way for media companies to survive is to own everything up and down the media chain—from broadcast and cable networks to the sitcoms, movies, and new broadcasts you see on those stations; to the production studios that make them; to the cable, satellite, and broadcast systems that bring the programs to your television set; to the Web sites you visit to read about those programs; to the way you log on to the Internet to view those pages. Big media today wants to own the faucet, pipeline, water, and the reservoir. The rain clouds come next.[13]

In recent years, a clear split has emerged among the five FCC commissioners, with the three Republicans voting for ever more deregulation and the two Democrats voting against this trend. One of the two dissenting voices belongs to Commissioner Michael Copps, a Democrat appointed by President George W. Bush. At a January 2003 forum at Columbia University, Copps explained the minority point of view:

> Why am I concerned? I don't believe that we have the foggiest idea right now about the potential consequences of our actions. We have a model to look at for what eliminating concentration protections might do to the media—the radio industry. Many believe that the elimination of radio consolidation rules created real problems. . . . Undoubtedly some efficiencies were created that allowed broadcast media companies to operate more profitably.

These efficiencies may even have kept some stations in business. But the consolidation went far beyond what anyone expected. Conglomerates now own dozens, even hundreds—and in one case, more than a thousand—stations all across the country. More and more programming originates hundreds of miles away from listeners and their communities. And there are 34 percent fewer radio station owners than there were before safeguards were eliminated. The majority of markets today are dominated by oligopoly. And all this in only a few years![14]

Does it matter? Does it matter if local voices are being replaced by those of huge, faceless, profit-driven corporations? Yes, and for a number of reasons. *Safety* is one issue. The thousand-station conglomerate that Copps refers to is Clear Channel Communications— yet another media giant, which has grown from a mere 40 stations in 1996 to more than 1,200 today. So how does safety come into play? Consider this report from the *New York Times*:

> Senator Byron Dorgan, Democrat of North Dakota, had a potential disaster in his district when a freight train carrying anhydrous ammonia derailed, releasing a deadly cloud over the city of Minot. When the emergency alert system failed, the police called the town radio stations, six of which are owned by the corporate giant Clear Channel. According to news accounts, no one answered the phone at the stations for more than an hour and a half. Three hundred people were hospitalized, some partially blinded by the ammonia. Pets and livestock were killed.[15]

Quality is another concern, as media giants swallow up the competition. A five-year study undertaken in 1998 by the Project for Excellence in Journalism looked at 22,000 stories aired on 172 TV news programs. Although the findings were mixed, overall, the data "strongly suggest regulatory changes that encourage heavy concentration of ownership in local television by a few large corporations will erode the quality of news Americans receive."[16]

Diversity is yet another important issue. Early in 2003, Senator John McCain introduced legislation to encourage minority ownership of media outlets. He pointed out at that time that as of December 2000, minorities represented 29 percent of the U.S. population and yet owned a mere 3.8 percent of commercial broadcast facilities.[17] And although FCC chairman Powell publicly applauded Senator McCain's efforts, nothing much changed on the policy side. In September 2003, for example, the FCC approved the merger between the Hispanic Broadcasting Corporation and Univision, creating a Spanish-language monolith that now effectively controls most of the key sources of information aimed at the Hispanic community in the United States.

Innovation is also in peril as a result of media consolidation. Ted Turner makes this point: the little guys—the upstarts—are the ones who force change upon their industry, simply because they have no other choice. The big guys hunker down and protect their interests.

And finally, *the public's right to know* is jeopardized. Republican congressman Mark Foley, who represents the Sixteenth Congressional District in the heart of Florida, used to count on local radio stations to help him stay in touch with his constituents. When the national media moved into his district, the number of local stations plummeted from five to one.[18]

Is democracy on the block? Yes. The question is, What are we going to do about it?

MICHAEL MOORE MEETS MICKEY MOUSE

As noted above, the Sinclair Broadcast Group decided that *Nightline*'s plan to read the names and show the pictures of American servicemen and -women killed in Iraq was politically motivated. "We find it to be contrary to public interest," commented Sinclair's general counsel Barry Faber.[19]

Thankfully, given its behaviors, Sinclair isn't one of the really big players in the media industry, where today just five companies— Time Warner, Disney (ABC), General Electric (NBC Universal), News Corporation (Fox), and Viacom (CBS)—collectively control something like *80 percent* of the video content of the country.

So now let's look at an example of how a truly big media company can throw its weight around. Let's look at the Walt Disney Company's celebrated decision, in the spring of 2004, to deep-six Michael Moore's *Fahrenheit 9/11*.

Ask people on the street what they think of when they hear the word *Disney*, and you're likely to hear about cartoon characters, favorite movies, and theme parks. I'd bet that only a relatively small percentage of the general populace know that Disney owns (for example) the American Broadcasting Company—the same ABC that ran afoul of the Sinclair Broadcast Group, earlier in this chapter—and (according to the *Columbia Journalism Review*) all of the following properties as well:

• **Publishing companies:** Hyperion, Disney Publishing Worldwide, Hyperion Books for Children, and Disney Global Children's Books, as well as various related imprints
• **Magazines:** *Automotive Industries, Biography* (with GE and Hearst), *Discover, Disney Adventures, Disney Magazine, ECN News, ESPN Magazine* (distributed by Hearst), *Family Fun, Institutional Investor, JCK, Kodin, Top Famille, US Weekly* (a 50 percent share), *Video Business,* and *Quality*
• **A television network** (ABC, the acquisition of which in 1995 marked a major turning point for the expansionist Disney company)
• **Owned and operated television stations** (in Chicago, Flint, Fresno, Houston, Los Angeles, New York City, Philadelphia, Raleigh/Durham, San Francisco, and Toledo)
• **Radio stations:** sixty-four in all, including two in Atlanta, four in Chicago, five in Dallas, three in Detroit, four in Los Angeles, *six* in Minneapolis–Saint Paul, four in New York City, three in Washington, D.C., and the list goes on and on, also including Radio Disney and ESPN Radio's syndicated programming
• **Cable television:** ABC Family, the Disney Channel, Toon Disney, SoapNet, ESPN Inc. (an 80 percent share) and all its various spin-offs, Classic Sports Network, A&E Television (a 37.5 percent share), the History Channel (a partial share), Lifetime Television (a 50 percent share), Lifetime Movie Network (a 50 percent share), and E! Entertainment (a partial share)

• **International broadcasting operations:** Disney Channels in the UK, Taiwan, Australia, Malaysia, France, the Middle East, Italy, and Spain; ESPN Inc. International Ventures; Sportsvision of Australia (a 25 percent share); ESPN Brazil (a 50 percent share); ESPN STAR (a 50 percent share); and Net STAR (a 33 percent share)

• **Other international ventures,** including television production and distribution companies in Germany and France, TV Sport of France, Tesauro of Spain, Scandinavian Broadcasting System, and the Japan Sports Channel

• **Television production and distribution:** Buena Vista Television, Touchstone Television, Walt Disney Television, and Walt Disney Television Animation, which owns production facilities in Japan, Australia, and Canada

• **Movie production and distribution:** Walt Disney Pictures, Touchstone Pictures, Hollywood Pictures, Caravan Pictures, Miramax Films—to which we'll return shortly!—Buena Vista Home Video, Buena Vista Home Entertainment, and Buena Vista International

• **Financial and retail:** a partial interest in Sid R. Bass, and the Disney Stores

• **Walt Disney Internet Group:** ABC Internet Group, ABC.com, ABCNEWS.com, Oscar.com, Mr. Showbiz, Disney Online, Disney's Daily Blast, Disney.com, Family.com, ESPN Internet Group, ESPN.sportzone.com, Soccernet.com (a 60 percent share), NBA.com, NASCAR.com, Skillgames, Wall of Sound, Go Network, and a majority stake in Toysmart.com

• **Music:** Buena Vista Music Group, Hollywood Records, Lyric Street Records, Mammoth Records, and Walt Disney Records

• **Theater and sports:** Walt Disney Theatrical Productions and Anaheim Sports

• And, of course, **theme parks and resorts:** Disneyland, Disney-MGM Studios, Disneyland Paris, Disney Regional Entertainment, Disneyland Resort, Disney Vacation Club, Epcot, Magic Kingdom, Tokyo Disneyland (a partial share), Walt Disney World, Disney's Animal Kingdom, Walt Disney World Sports Complex, Disney Cruise Line, and the Disney Institute[20]

This lengthy list is reproduced here for two reasons. First, it's important to underscore the vast scope of the Disney enterprises today, both vertical and horizontal, and suggest to you the extent to which—even if you have never set foot in Walt Disney World and don't intend to—CEO Bob Iger's empire is already a factor in your life. Second, it's important to put the tug of war between Disney and Michael Moore in context. You have to picture a *really big* Goliath and a *really small* David.

The story begins in May 2003, when Disney subsidiary Miramax signs up to produce (that is, finance) filmmaker Michael Moore's latest jeremiad: this one about the alleged shortcomings and conflicting agendas of the presidency of George W. Bush. Moore, of course, is already well-known for his documentaries (some would say "mockumentaries") bedeviling corporate moguls (*Roger and Me*) and the gun lobby (*Bowling for Columbine*). The latter film, which cost distributor United Artists a mere $3 million to make, raked in something like $120 million in box office receipts and DVD sales and rentals. Not surprisingly, Moore—also selling a lot of books in the same vein, and showing up regularly on the hippest TV talk shows—is considered a hot property.

Miramax, for its part, inhabits the adventurous end of the normally bland Disney spectrum. In recent years, it has cranked out a large number of quality entries, such as *Shakespeare in Love* and *The Aviator*. Miramax is the brainchild of Bob and Harvey Weinstein, who in the early nineties sold out to Disney but remained in charge of the business. (Harvey Weinstein, it should be noted, is a major contributor to Democrats and the Democratic Party, while Disney's Eisner—Weinstein's ultimate boss—is a prominent backer of Republicans.) One of the few material terms of the agreement was that Disney reserved the right to prevent its new subsidiary from distributing films that ran over budget or that earned the dreaded NC-17 rating.[21]

When the Miramax-Moore deal was first announced in May 2003, the conservative lobby went to work on Disney CEO Eisner, trying to get the contract negated. According to Moore's agent, Ari Emanuel, Eisner asked Emanuel in advance *not* to cut a deal with

Miramax. Once the deal was done, Emanuel later recollected, Eisner asked him to undo it. According to the *New York Times:*

> Mr. Emanuel said Mr. Eisner expressed particular concern that it would endanger tax breaks Disney receives for its theme park, hotels, and other ventures in Florida, where Mr. Bush's brother, Jeb, is governor. "Michael Eisner asked me not to sell this movie to Harvey Weinstein; that doesn't mean I listened to him," Mr. Emanuel said. "He definitely indicated that there were tax incentives he was getting for the Disney corporation and that's why he didn't want me to sell to Miramax. He didn't want a Disney company involved."[22]

Disney officials subsequently confirmed that they didn't want the film in the first place, although they denied linking the Moore contract with the Florida tax-break issue. In any case, the deal between Moore and Miramax was cut. Conservatives continued to grumble. Eisner, presumably, continued to wish the deal would go away.

Why? Well, for one thing, the Florida state employees' pension fund—of which Governor Jeb Bush was a trustee—held some 7.3 million shares of Disney. For another, Disney's unique relationship with the state of Florida gave it near-feudal control over 40,000 acres of land in the Orlando area. And for another, the Bush brothers gave public votes of confidence to Disney at key junctures. In the wake of 9/11, for example, President Bush urged anxious Americans to "go down to Disney World in Florida. Take your families and enjoy life." Over the 2002 Christmas holidays, the president, his brother, and more than a dozen other Bush family members took a conspicuous cruise on the then-struggling Disney Cruise Line.[23]

The next major development in the story came on May 4, 2004. That's the day, according to Michael Moore, on which his agent and Miramax were informed that Disney was taking steps to block the release of *Fahrenheit 9/11.* "It's not in the interest of any major corporation," one Disney executive explained to the *Times,* "to be dragged into a highly charged partisan political battle."[24]

Moore, on his Web site, expressed outrage:

Some people may be afraid of this movie because of what it will show. But there's nothing they can do about it now because it's done, it's awesome, and if I have anything to say about it, you'll see it this summer—because, after all, it is a free country.[25]

The *New York Times,* editorializing the next day, condemned what it called "Disney's Craven Behavior":

Give the Walt Disney Company a gold medal for cowardice for blocking its Miramax division from distributing a film that criticizes President Bush and his family. A company that ought to be championing free expression has instead chosen to censor a documentary that clearly falls within the bounds of acceptable political commentary. . . . [If Florida tax breaks are] the reason for Disney's move, it would underscore the dangers of allowing huge conglomerates to gobble up diverse media companies.

On the other hand, a senior Disney executive says the real reason is that Disney caters to families of all political stripes and that many of them might be alienated by the film. Those families, of course, would not have to watch the documentary.

It is hard to say which rationale for blocking distribution is more depressing. But it is clear that Disney loves its bottom line more than the freedom of political discourse.[26]

You may have followed the rest of the story. Moore's movie—a scathing, partisan, tragicomic indictment of the Bush administration—began getting rave reviews from preview audiences. At the end of May 2004, *Fahrenheit 9/11* won the Palme d'Or at the Cannes Film Festival: one of the highest honors in filmmaking, and one which hadn't gone to a documentary since a 1956 Jacques Cousteau film. A few days later, the Weinstein brothers of Miramax personally bought the rights to *Fahrenheit 9/11* for around $6 million—the costs incurred up to that point—and began arranging for last-minute theatrical distribution. The film set records on its opening weekend and, by mid-August, had grossed $155 million worldwide.[27]

Although firestorms erupted over the accuracy of the allegations in the film (which Moore persisted in calling a "comedy"), the consensus was that at least in its broad brushstrokes, *Fahrenheit 9/11* was reasonably factual. "It seems safe to say," wrote one *Times* reviewer, "that central assertions of fact in 'Fahrenheit 9/11' are supported by the public record (indeed, many of them will be familiar to those who have closely followed Mr. Bush's political career.)"[28] A reviewer in the normally conservative *New York Daily News* called the film "a soaring display of American patriotism" and a "loud celebration of our great Bill of Rights."[29]

So what do we take away from this sorry saga? For one thing, we see what happens when an enormous media conglomerate uses its considerable clout in the marketplace—a clout that has resulted in large part from *vertical* integration—to advance its political agenda. If you own both the production and the distribution ends of your industry, you're in a pretty good position to call the shots. (Didn't we deregulate the electric industry to prevent exactly this sort of vertical integration from happening?) Disney and the others in the Big Five make the stuff, and then they have the luxury of deciding how and where to use it, regardless of the public's need to know. And in that way, they help shape public opinion—and, arguably, help determine the outcome of the next election.

Now, just for argument's sake, let's imagine that cable giant Comcast had succeeded in its effort to acquire Disney. (So far, I haven't even touched upon the enormous power of the five cable giants.) Today, 42 percent of cable networks are vertically integrated with either a cable operator or a satellite company. If Comcast/Disney had happened—and the deal might yet come back to life—this vertical integration percentage would have risen to almost 50 percent. That's how big these deals are getting, and how far this integration has proceeded.

So the other lesson here involves the perils of *horizontal* integration, especially in the media field. Remember that list of Disney enterprises from earlier in the chapter—everything from books to boats? When a media company gets into enough activities, its calculation of its responsibilities becomes much more complicated. The prospect of losing tax breaks (or favorable zoning regulations, or the inflow of public pension-fund dollars, or product endorsements from the president and your most important governor) simply overwhelms the public trust that is inherent in the media field. "Serving the public interest" gives way to "protecting our corporate interests." The desire to avoid unwanted scrutiny travels in the garb of avoiding conflicts of interest.

"I would prefer [that] ABC not cover Disney," Michael Eisner announced, shortly after buying the network. Well, sure; so would I, if I were Eisner, riding herd over a sprawling empire that, if only because of the law of averages, is almost certain to make a decision sooner or later that doesn't stand up very well under media scrutiny. The fact that ABC's *20/20* news program killed a show critical of Disney a few days after Eisner's announcement should give us all pause.[30]

Justice Louis Brandeis, writing in the 1927 *Whitney v. California* case, put it neatly:

> Those who won our independence believed that the final end of the State was to make men free to develop their faculties; . . . that the greatest menace to freedom is an inert people; that public discussion is a political duty; and that this should be a fundamental principle of American government.[31]

In August 2003, Arnold Schwarzenegger announced his candidacy for the governorship of California on Jay Leno's *Tonight Show* (owned by NBC, owned by General Electric). Where were the more than fifty other candidates that night? And two months later, at his postvictory celebration, Schwarzenegger was introduced to a national TV audience by none other than Jay Leno (owned by NBC, owned by General Electric).

Are we "inert," in Brandeis's sense of the word? We're getting there. Is our democracy on the block? Absolutely. And it's going to take a concerted effort on the part of some CEOs—working with key legislators, angry citizens, and a new crop of regulators—to get it back off the block.

5

CEO COMPENSATION: WHAT'S WRONG, WHAT'S RIGHT

Do you think people should be paid what they're worth?

Careful, it's a trick question. If you're a CEO in the United States today—and to some extent, elsewhere in the world—you're probably overpaid. So you may not want to answer this question.

In this chapter, we'll consider appropriate levels and methods of compensation for CEOs and other high-ranking corporate executives. It's a topic that has received a lot of attention in recent months. It's also one that I feel very passionately about, so I want to put my two cents in. Maybe the fact that I've been a CEO and gotten rich in the process—in ways that I think hold up pretty well under scrutiny—will give my two cents a little extra currency.

THE STARTING POINT

Let's start at the beginning, with Compensation 101.

CEOs get four kinds of pay: salary, bonuses, stock options, and boodle (which I'll define shortly). Back in the good old days of American capitalism—say, sixty years ago—CEOs didn't make all that much from any of these kinds of pay, or even from all of them put together.

The cash side of the story was relatively straightforward.

Salaries—the first leg of the four-legged compensation stool—tended to be modest. Looking back a half century or more, your typical CEO made about twice as much as your typical president of the United States. You could argue that President Eisenhower was underpaid, but his counterparts in the private sector probably weren't overpaid.

Back in those good old days, bonuses tended to be tied to extraordinary performance, and since no one is extraordinary every year, few CEOs got enormous bonuses every year. A bonus was in fact a *bonus*—something extra that you got when your company either met high expectations or far exceeded ho-hum expectations.

There was one notable exception to this rule. Some companies went the route of defining "automatic" management bonuses that would be awarded if certain year-over-year performance goals were met. Not surprisingly, this development led to lots of gaming of the system: *Hold on to earnings until the appropriate reporting period, beat the hell out of your vendors as necessary, whip your sales force to deliver the right numbers at the right time,* and so on, and so on. In light of recent events, it's ironic that the remedy that these companies eventually settled upon to address this problem—stock options—led to even greater problems.

Options—the equity side of the story—were a kind of retirement plan in disguise. They tended to be handed out only to a select few. Coming into your senior position, you'd be given an opportunity to buy your blue-chip company's stock sometime in the distant future at a price that was fixed today. Since you were expected to remain with the company for many, many years, and since the stock was expected to rise gradually over those years, you would ultimately derive a nice benefit. Many a college education was funded through gifts of Grandpa's appreciated stock, which Grandpa had accumulated in this relatively genteel way.

Options were also intended as a way of aligning the interests of management with the interests of the shareholders. Back in the days of the robber barons, the managers *were* the shareholders. (Think Andrew Carnegie.) But as the managerial class arose toward the end of the nineteenth century, accompanied by a much broader base of stock ownership, there also arose the challenge of making this new breed of samurai do the right thing by their masters, the absentee owners. Eventually, the device of options was invented to help the samurai keep their eyes on the ball and think about the long-term needs of the company

But somewhere along the way, something funny happened to options. In the good old days, if an option went "underwater"—if the company's share price sagged so much that the option was no longer worth anything—the CEO who held the option was out of luck. No big payday. Then came the magic of "reloading" options, meaning that the company would revalue the options in such a way as to make them motivational to the CEO again. That's like sending in the field-goal kicker, and—after he fails to reach the crossbar—moving the goalposts in twenty yards and giving him another shot.

Now we come to *boodle,* one of my favorite words, which I'll define as "a large amount of money that has been acquired or used in an improper way." Earlier, we looked at the example of Dennis Kozlowski, who spent obscene amounts of money gratifying himself and his girlfriend.[1] One of Kozlowski's Christmas parties allegedly set the company back $50,000 in flowers and lavish gratuities alone.[2]

In recent years, of course, things have changed dramatically on at least three of the four compensation fronts: salaries, options, and boodle. Today, your average CEO makes more than *sixty-two times* as much as your average U.S. president.[3] And since we're paying our presidents a little better than we did back in Ike's day, that means we're paying our CEOs a *whole lot* better. And it's not as if only the Johnsons, Nixons, Fords, and so on fell behind. Everybody fell behind our CEOs and their princely pay scales:

> If the average pay for factory workers had grown at the same rate as it has for CEOs, their 1999 earnings would have been $114,035, rather than $23,753. If the minimum wage had risen as fast as CEO pay, it would now be $24.13 per hour, instead of $5.15 (which in real dollars is a decline from the 1970 level).[4]

But buried in these statistics is another kind of shift that has had enormous implications over the past decade or so. CEO pay has been skewed upward enormously by the huge increase in the frequency, scale, and value of options awards. Mainly during the go-go 1990s, options were transformed from the sleepy tool of Grandpa's day into the high-octane jet fuel of the Great American Bubble Economy.

In the headiest days of Silicon Valley, options were in fact the *only* way to go. Back then, you wouldn't consider joining a high-tech start-up without a serious equity stake. Options were transformed into a hot currency, and equally important, the way people thought about options was transformed. They were no longer a building block in a retirement plan; now, they were *how I'm going to buy that island next year and also the yacht I'll need to sail over to it.*

There is one other important aspect to the options game. From the company's perspective, options had a sort of magical quality. The Financial and Accounting Standards Board (FASB) sets the standards for U.S. corporate accounting. Because FASB didn't require companies to show the cost of options anywhere on their income statements, mainly for political reasons to which we'll return shortly, options were (or at least seemed to be) free money. A company could hand out options like candy corn—whether for recruitment or retention purposes—and make only passing reference to them in a footnote, somewhere: *Oh, yeah, lest we forget—we handed out some options last year. Didn't cost us anything, though.*

This book won't go too deeply into a discussion of options. Why? First, it's a complicated, controversial realm, with few easy answers. Second, FASB and other regulatory bodies are now tightening the rules. And finally, increasing numbers of companies are already doing the right thing by assigning a reasonable value to their options and expensing them.

But at the same time, options are not yesterday's news. Entrepreneurial hot spots like Silicon Valley absolutely depend on options. (Pick your metaphor: jet fuel, lubricant, whatever.) When you're in the business of making something from nothing—or to phrase it more charitably, of turning a vision into a going concern—you need a way to capture the expected value of that future enterprise. Jolt Cola and Twinkies may keep the twentysomethings working all night, but your thirtysomethings need numbers with lots of zeros next to them. Options are a tool for capturing tomorrow's hoped-for reality. The well-wired high-tech crowd loves them. And since options won't go away, we have to concentrate on making them work right—a subject for later in the chapter.

And finally, there's boodle. I've noticed something interesting: when a CEO (or a politician, for that matter) persists in having extra women in his life, there's usually boodle in the vicinity. We've already determined that these guys aren't hurting for money, so it's not a financial issue. Boodle is a sign that our guy is out of control. He's started to believe his own PR. He's started to believe that the company's fate rests in his hands. He's started to believe that he's an Olympian, walking among mere mortals.

"The way I calculate it," Dennis Kozlowski told *Business Week,* "while I gained $139 million, I created about $37 billion in wealth for our shareholders." Well, seen in *that* light, who cares if there's a girlfriend on the side, and if more than a million in shareholder assets get steered in her direction in the form of lavish gifts and entertainment?[5]

But as Kozlowski found out, we mortals do care, especially if it's *our* assets that are being missteered.

We're especially annoyed when we read studies that suggest that, at the end of the day, most CEOs have only a marginal impact on the fate of their companies. What really counts are things like larger economic trends, the skill level of your workforce, and how well your products or services meet some sort of need in the marketplace. Sure, CEOs make key decisions in the realm of mergers, acquisitions, and divestitures (although the evidence suggests that, ultimately, many of these moves actually destroy shareholder wealth even as they increase executive compensation). And yes, CEOs make critical decisions today that have enormous long-term implications: *We're going to put our R & D dollars here rather than there,* for example. But CEOs are far from omniscient or omnipotent, and they don't deserve to be treated as if they were. And they certainly have no right to turn my money or your money into boodle.

This book is only incidentally a history, but the reader may already be asking an obvious question: *What went wrong?* When and why did CEOs get such big heads about themselves? Jim Collins, author of *Built to Last* and *Good to Great,* attributes the deification of CEOs in the United States—and their outlandish compensation packages—to a single event: the publication in July 1986 of Lee Iacocca's self-aggrandizing autobiography, *Iacocca.* Before that time, CEOs weren't a particularly interesting topic of conversation; after *Iacocca,* things went bad quickly. People couldn't get enough gossip about business potentates. Even worse, boards started looking for celebrity CEOs. Worse yet, people who liked to be gossiped about starting gunning for the corner office, and people who didn't want to conduct themselves like pop stars started steering clear of the job.[6]

Of course, there were many other factors at work, including the larger trivialization of our culture, and the long-running economic boom (and the intensive supply-side propaganda) that began in the later years of the Reagan administration. But hey, I'm willing to blame Iacocca, if Jim Collins is.[7]

LIVING THE GOOD LIFE AT COMPUTER ASSOCIATES

One of the most amazing stories of wretched excess, in the realm of CEO and senior executive compensation, comes from Islandia, New York. This is the home of Computer Associates International Inc., a leading manufacturer of software that helps huge companies manage their computer networks.

In 1995, Computer Associates (CA) was headed by the troika of Charles Wang (founder and CEO), Sanjay Kumar (chief operating officer), and Russell Artzt (executive vice president). In that year, CA's board put an interesting bogey on the table, intended to motivate these three guys. The board offered a five-year contract under which Wang, Kumar, and Artzt would receive a total of 20.3 million shares in free CA stock if the share price went up by at least 20 percent—and stayed there for at least sixty days—during that five-year period.

Laid out on the page like that, that's a staggering proposition. What in the world was that board thinking? Sure, it was an ambitious goal. But if the troika hit that goal, it would be monstrously expensive to the company. And by the way, with such a huge payoff looming, wouldn't CA's executives be under extraordinary pressure to make the numbers come out right, one way or the other?

In 1999, the bill came due. Wang received $655.4 million in pay and exercised options, making him the highest-paid CEO in the United States—probably the highest-paid CEO in the history of the galaxy. Kumar got $359 million, and Artzt had to settle for $129 million. The total damages: more than $1.1 billion. CA had to take out loans totaling $675 million to pay the bill, which wiped out almost half of the company's profits from the previous three years.[8]

When news of this fiasco leaked out, CA's stock plunged more than 30 percent. In other words, we tell the Big Three that we're going to pay them a king's ransom to juice up our stock price. The sector goes white-hot over the next few years (with the S&P tech-stock index going up an average of 24 percent per year), meaning that external forces have lowered and widened the crossbar and moved the goalposts well within reach of almost anybody who could put his big toe into the ball. Then when they put the ball over the crossbar, we have to take out a huge loan, and the stock plummets.

Not surprisingly, shareholders howled, and the three bucca-neers eventually turned some of their stock (about 4.5 million shares) back in to the company. Wang's paycheck shrank by about $144.5 million, which meant that he only earned a half-billion dollars in 1999. At first, Wang wasn't too concerned. "I know my directors," as he reportedly said to *Business Week*. "They'll make me whole again."

The real punch line on this sordid story may be yet to come. In the later months of 2001, the SEC announced that it was looking into the possibility that top executives at CA inflated the company's reported sales and profits in order to hit that billion-dollar payday. When a grand jury was empaneled in Brooklyn a year later, Charles Wang immediately retired—a coincidence of timing, according to a company spokesperson.

Rumors flew concerning how CA's senior management had

been trying to use creative accounting to rewrite the history of the company's spectacular growth.[9] But the prosecutors had more than rumors to work with. For one thing, CA couldn't seem to get its numbers straight. In 2000, for example, the company restated its 1999 revenues: down from $2.13 billion to $1.91 billion. Why? It seems they had counted some contracts twice. (Hey, it happens: a hundred million here, a hundred million there.) And in May 2001, CA issued a hurried restatement of its profits for the year ended March 2001. Seems profits weren't actually $230 million, as announced only a month earlier, but more like $90 million.[10] In October 2003, an internal committee set up by the company criticized its leaders for "prematurely" booking revenues; this move prompted the departure of CA's chief financial officer and two of his top staffers.[11]

Gradually, under pressure from the regulators and prosecutors, CA broomed itself out. Sanjay Kumar, who briefly succeeded the disgraced Charles Wang as chairman and CEO, left the company in June 2004. It was almost business as usual, according to a press release issued by the company's reconfigured board:

> The Board wishes Sanjay and his family well. The Board is committed to reaching a settlement of the government's investigation into the Company's past accounting practices as quickly as possible. We are working hard to take the remedial steps necessary to put this entire matter behind CA. Sanjay's decision to leave CA was made in that spirit.[12]

Sounds friendly enough. But on his way out the door, according to regulatory filings made later by the company, Kumar was compelled to leave behind $7.56 million in restricted stock; 565,600 unexercised options; and, possibly, a $1 million bonus and severance payment.[13] Then a major shareholder filed suit against CA's former executives in an effort to recover their extraordinary payouts. And then shareholders introduced a proposal to require the company to recoup performance-based executive compensation when, in hindsight, the restatement of financial results made such compensation inappropriate.[14] As of this writing, the SEC has yet to reach its judgment in the CA case, but whatever it is, it's not likely to be a happy one for the shareholders.

Why report at length on such a clear-cut case of wretched excess? The sheer extremeness of the story makes an important point. It's astounding that CA's board could have cut the deal it did. It's astounding that the entire top management of a reputable company would have agreed to it, apparently without any reservations whatsoever. It's astounding that when the huge payday came, the board didn't ask for a renegotiation of the deal, and instead the company took out an enormous loan to pay the bill that was coming due (thereby wiping out what amounted to a year and a half of corporate profits and knocking the pins out from under the share price). It's astounding that Wang, Kumar, and the rest didn't look at themselves in the mirror and say, *This is wrong!*

Or at least, *We'll never get away with this!*

But they didn't look in that mirror. And the result, predictably, was mutiny on the part of shareholders. In 1992, the SEC ruled that shareholder resolutions regarding executive compensation could no longer be considered business-as-usual issues and therefore could no longer be excluded from proxy statements. In other words, the SEC put a significant cudgel in the hand of shareholders. But it wasn't until the likes of Wang and Kumar, and their counterparts at other companies, roused their shareholders—really ticked them off—that shareholders decided to pick up that cudgel.

Better late than never.

WATCH THAT RATIO

The CA story is about a company's losing its moral compass. And it's about the dark side of human nature asserting itself.

There's a good reason why the Lord's Prayer implores God not to lead us into temptation: most of us aren't very well equipped to resist it. That being said, CEOs do have to provide their company's moral compass. This is not something that they're going to learn how to do after they get the job. So that means, in turn, that a major part of the board's deliberations, when it comes to picking a new CEO, ought to revolve around the candidate's perceived integrity. When temptation rolls out on the table, what's this individual likely to do?

Let's look at some of the things that a CEO can and should do to make sure that his or her compensation is appropriate and that it will reinforce his or her role as the leader of the business.

The first thing is to watch that ratio—the relationship between the highest-paid and the lowest-paid people in the organization. The bigger the spread, the less likely that the CEO's pay is justifiable—and the more likely that he or she will lose credibility and respect.

Let me cite some personal history to make this point. When I graduated from Stanford Business School in 1971, I landed a job with a mining company called Utah International. I didn't have any burning desire to go into the extractive-industry field; the real draw in that job was Utah's CEO, a very interesting and wonderfully capable executive named Ed Littlefield. He had gone to Stanford in the thirties, and every two years he hired a Stanford MBA to be his assistant. Around Stanford, this was known to be one of the two great jobs you could get—the other being at Cummins Engine—and I felt extremely lucky to have landed it.

Ed Littlefield, it turned out, was one of the best individuals and greatest business leaders I've ever had the privilege of meeting. My starting salary was $15,600. Ed's salary—available for all to see, since UI was a public company—was $150,000. So the ratio between Ed's salary and mine was about 10:1. Now, I wasn't the lowest-paid person in the organization, but I doubt whether there was anybody at UI who was making less than $9,000 on a full-time basis. So let's say the spread between the top and the bottom of the ladder was 16:1, and the spread between Littlefield's salary and that of the average employee was significantly smaller.

Now consider the fact that the spread between the pay of Cisco's CEO John Chambers and that of his average employee is 2,300:1. Chambers represents a somewhat extreme case, but there are an awful lot of extreme cases out there:

In 1980, the median CEO pay package was about $1 million.
This rose to over $7 million by 2001 (measured in 2001 dollars).

To put this into perspective, in the two decades since 1980 the pay of the average rank-and-file worker increased (in inflation-adjusted terms) by about 15 percent, while CEO pay increased by nearly 600 percent. The average ratio of total CEO pay to average worker pay increased from about 50 in 1980 to about 500 in 2001.[15]

This is way out of whack. CEOs aren't worth that much. Michael Eisner—whom we met in our last chapter—was paid $800 million by Disney over a thirteen-year period. In that period, he delivered returns to his investors that were less than they would have gotten from investing the same money in T-bonds. And Eisner is considered by some to be a *good* CEO.[16] If you go looking for bad CEOs, the story is far worse.

Forbes found one: Richard A. Manoogian, who has headed bathroom-and-kitchen-cabinetmaker MASCO Corporation for thirty-six years. Over the past six years, he has paid himself an average of $13 million and earned an average 2 percent annually for his shareholders.[17]

Yes, CEOs are a commodity, and companies have to go out into their particular marketplace and purchase that commodity. So there's no one-size-fits-all ratio. But boards simply have to stop ratcheting up CEO pay into ever-higher levels of the stratosphere (and in the process, ratcheting up all those executives one or two levels down in the organization). Impossible, you say? Well, it's worth pointing out that boards in other countries somehow find a way to stay out of this trap: even without taking options and bonuses into account, your average CEO in the United States is paid more than twice as much as his or her counterpart in other industrialized nations.[18] And as Ed Littlefield's example certainly illustrates, it wasn't so long ago that CEOs were paid relatively modest salaries in *this* country.

Boards need to worry about ways of closing the gap, and they should start closing it by working on the other end of the ladder. I'll have more to say about this later in this chapter, and also in subsequent chapters. For now, though, I'll offer one proposal: *if you're paying your top executives too much, cut their pay and redistribute that excess.* Sometimes when I suggest this, people simply back away from me like I'm crazy. But other people respond that such a move would be merely a symbolic gesture—one that would punish the big guy without really helping the little guy.

Not so. If the "CEO tax" (that is, the excessive compensation) paid by Occidental Petroleum in 1997 had been distributed across that huge company's workforce, everybody would have gotten an extra $8,199. And if the excessive compensation paid to other top Occidental executives had been similarly redistributed, everybody would have gotten an additional $16,398![19]

How many average Joes at Occidental would have turned up their noses at an extra sixteen grand? Not too many. And lest we forget, those are the people who actually *earned* most of that money for the company.

SHARE THE WEALTH

A second general piece of advice about CEO compensation: *share the wealth*—if necessary, even before you have it.

When I took over TCI in February 1997, the company had something like 35,000 employees. I was surprised to discover that only about thirty-five managers at any level received compensation over and above their salaries. It seemed to me that a) this wasn't a very bright scheme for motivating all of our roughly 650 managers, and b) it was absurd to think that the tiny circle of 35 embraced every manager who was making a significant contribution to the business. So I immediately broadened that benefit to include all 650 managers. Not perfect, but certainly much better.

Meanwhile, I started looking at the equity side of the equation. In February 1997, TCI's stock was bouncing along the bottom, at something like eleven and three-eighths, which was essentially an all-time low. I decided that we weren't going anywhere unless everybody felt like he or she personally would benefit from a dramatic appreciation in the stock price. So I worked out a deal whereby we gave everyone in the company an additional bump of between 10 and 15 percent of his or her salary in the form of company stock, deposited in each individual's 401(k) retirement account.

We CEOs have a proven talent for deluding ourselves—witness all those tales of poor performance and high compensation mentioned above—but I am convinced that this single gesture, which was not all that expensive to the company, made a huge difference in our subsequent history. Yes, people were working for me, and for TCI, but they were also working for themselves, and that prompted a huge psychological shift. Within just twenty-five months, when I closed the sale of TCI to AT&T, our stock had appreciated fivefold, and everybody—shareholders and all employees alike—made a fortune.

I certainly didn't invent this idea. The progressive Michigan-based furniture maker Herman Miller, for example, was one of many companies to establish an employee stock-ownership plan in the mid-1980s.[20] (Employees became owners in that company after a year of service.) There were lots of other ESOPs, of various stripes and flavors, before we did our thing at TCI. Most companies that adopt them swear by them.

Nor was I being selfless. Motivating 35,000 people to work their hardest and their smartest helped make me rich (and did right by our shareholders too). And frankly, if anyone complained about how rich our senior executives were getting, it was really nice to be able to say, "Hey, pal, a whole lot of other really good people were along for the ride too."

One more idea from the annals of TCI, again inspired by my mentor Ed Littlefield: I paid all of my VPs exactly the same salary. Period. And I tended to err on the high side. On the former point, I didn't want people focusing on politics; I wanted them focused on performance. Getting the VP cohort to stop worrying about a $10,000 differential between Jack's salary and Jill's salary turned out to be enormously liberating for all concerned. As for the latter point, well, I rarely had anybody come in and claim they were worth more than I was paying, and I like to think that a couple of underperformers either cranked up their productivity or were embarrassed enough to take themselves out of the game. In any case, I sure didn't waste much of *my* time worrying about individual VP compensation.

Let's return briefly to the subject of options, this time looking at prescriptions. First, and most important, *options should be expensed*. Back in 1992, the Financial Accounting Standards Board (FASB) concluded that options should be treated like any other corporate expense, meaning that they should be subtracted from the company's profits, thereby revealing a more accurate picture of those profits. But intensive lobbying by the CEO community, especially those from Silicon Valley, prevented this rule from being implemented at that time.

The plague of scandals at the turn of the twenty-first century created some renewed interest in this obvious and overdue reform. In March 2004, FASB once again decided in favor of expensing options, twelve years after its first run at the subject. Three financial heavyweights—Treasury secretary John W. Snow, SEC chairman William H. Donaldson, and Fed chairman Alan Greenspan—also voiced their strong support for expensing options. But to the astonishment of many, the House voted in July 2004 against the option reform package in the Stock Option Accounting Reform Act, by something like a three-to-one margin. House members apparently bought the rationale of the high-tech industry and its run-amok lobbyists, who argued that the industry's reported earnings would plummet and its financial reports would be *less* accurate if options were expensed.

No matter that some reasonably successful companies—like, say, Microsoft—already expense their options, and that the sky has not fallen in Redmond, Washington.

I continue to support expensing options. Congress should either do the right thing or get out of the way and let FASB do the right thing. Incidentally, the shareholders of Intel, Apple, HP, and many other leading high-tech companies agree. "Our board of directors is analyzing how best to satisfy the advisory vote of our stockholders regarding expensing of options," Intel commented in a July 2004 SEC filing.[21] I hope Intel is only waiting for clarification of the option-pricing models proposed by FASB and isn't stalling for time and thereby thwarting the clearly expressed wishes of its owners.

Second, *options cannot be allowed to vest on a short-term basis*. We need to get back to Grandpa's concept of options: as a tool for making the shareholders' long-term interests coincide with the CEO's long-term interest. True, statistics show that today's investors tend to flit from stock to stock like bees in a field of wildflowers. But here's a place where some good regulation can put a useful stake in the ground. SEC memo to investors: *You want to flit? Fine. Flit. But every company's option plan will still be looking to the long term.*

Third, *options cannot be allowed to reload.* Remember the field-goal analogy. No moving the goalposts. No rerunning the play. Hindery memo to CEO: *If you can't make it work based on your original options package, you should step aside and give someone else a shot.*

LIVING LIKE ROYALTY

Some CEOs, unfortunately, are going to continue to think of themselves as royalty and therefore will continue to live like kings (and the occasional queen).

My advice to them is *Pick your role models carefully.*

There was a massive outpouring of grief in the Netherlands when Queen Juliana died in March 2004. Although Juliana was one of the wealthiest women in the world, she lived a reasonably down-to-earth life. She had won over her fellow countrymen in the dark days at the end of World War II, and they were persuaded that she had their best interests at heart. You could say more or less the same thing about Britain's Queen Mum, who died in 2002.

Hindery memo to Prince Charles: *Your generation of royalty is unlikely to win similar accolades when your time comes.*

You can't lead if you don't command the respect of your followers. Sure, the power and trappings of the CEO's position guarantee that you'll command the first 5 percent of people's respect and loyalty. But you have to earn the rest. And this gets us back to where we started this chapter: you should be paid what you're worth. No more, no less.

6

A TALE OF THREE BOARDS

CEOs—powerful as they often are—don't operate in a vacuum. They work in a specific corporate context, which to a large extent is created by the company's board. So we need to spend some time talking about the responsibilities of boards. They are the people who hire, keep an eye on (or don't keep an eye on), and sometimes even fire the CEOs we're focusing on.

We'll look at two really bad boards that recently have made history: the WorldCom and Enron boards. The WorldCom story, at least pre-2002, is one of incompetence and lack of interest—the "fat, dumb, and happy" model of corporate governance. It would almost be comical—*Head of compensation committee awards himself sweetheart deal on corporate jet lease; forgets to tell fellow directors*—if the consequences hadn't been so terrible for so many thousands of investors and employees.

Enron constitutes a much darker story. You can make the case that Enron's directors knew, or should have known, what was going on. And if they knew, they should have blown the whistle.

Not all boards are bad, of course. I'll conclude this chapter with a brief description of the GE board, which—although it has sometimes hit its own bumps in the road—generally exemplifies good corporate governance.

What Your Board Is Supposed to Do

What, exactly, is a board of directors supposed to do? What is good corporate governance, as exercised by a board?

Most U.S. companies choose to incorporate in the state of Delaware, not necessarily for noble reasons. (It's cheap on the front end; they don't tax you much; and the rules tend to be very corporation-friendly.) Delaware's relevant law says that "the business and affairs of every corporation shall be managed by or under the direction of a board of directors."[1]

Well, in real life, boards almost never manage the business and affairs of a moderate-sized corporation. It's too complicated a job. The directors are part-timers, at best. They may or may not possess relevant industry experience. They may or may not have the financial background or technical savvy that is generally needed to participate in the day-to-day life of the corporation.

And by the way, if any board I worked for ever really tried to inject themselves into the direct management of the company—*ever*—I'd quit on the spot. The CEO is the boss, and everybody has to understand that. He or she is going to be held accountable if the ship goes up on the rocks, so he or she has to have undisputed authority over the helm. Under no circumstances can there be a confusion about, or a circumventing of, the senior chain of command.

On the other hand, the board is (or should be) the boss's boss. The directors hire, evaluate, and compensate the CEO. Working with the CEO, they set strategy, at least in general terms. They pass judgment on the CEO's major decisions, sometimes to the point of taking formal votes on given proposals. (Major capital expenditures are typically put to a vote.) Through its system of committees, the board looks after issues of critical importance to stockholders and other external constituencies. The audit committee, which is now mandated by the stock exchanges and the SEC, works with the outside auditors to come up with "independent" assessments of the company's financial health; the compensation committee (mandated by the SEC) worries about senior-management compensation.[2] Committee work is about as hands-on as a board normally

gets. Committee roles and responsibilities have gotten a lot of attention in recent years—and deservedly so, as we'll see.

Less formally, the directors provide the CEO with an informal
sounding board—a sort of friendly critical voice—and in some
cases play a conscience-of-the-corporation role. What do I mean by
this? Simply put, it's all too easy for the CEO (even the best-
intentioned CEO) to get snared in the minutiae of management.
After all, the CEO, along with his or her leadership team, has to
focus on the short term, the middle term, and the long term. And
while this sounds pretty comprehensive, it still leaves a lot of terri-
tory uncovered.

One of my favorite stories in this regard comes from Cummins
Engine Company. In 1971, longtime board chairman J. Irwin
Miller challenged the chief operating officer, the estimable Jim
Henderson, to come up with a comprehensive corporate policy regarding the hiring of Vietnam veterans. This was not a departure,
in and of itself; most companies (including Cummins) had some
rules giving preferential treatment to veterans. But Miller told Henderson that the revised policy should cover not only veterans with
honorable discharges, but also people "who for reasons of conscience served jail terms" and "persons who for conscientious acts
received dishonorable discharges."[3]

In other words, what aren't we worrying about that we need to
be worrying about? Is there a broader picture here—a picture that
other people are missing? Where do our corporate (and individual)
responsibilities lie?

One more story in this vein: In the late 1980s, furniture maker
Herman Miller Inc. needed to consolidate its warehousing and distribution activities into a single centralized facility. (It was then
packing and shipping out of seven different buildings in western
Michigan.) A team of senior executives came up with a plan for
putting up a preengineered facility on a forty-acre site that the company owned. Speed was of the essence, they argued; too many ship-
ments were going out late or incomplete, and payments were
similarly being delayed. Board chairman Max DePree, who knew a
thing or two about the importance of getting corporate architec-
ture right, blew the whistle.

"Now that's a perfectly good cornfield," he told the executives at a board meeting. "We had better be sure we know *exactly* what we're doing before we mess it up."[4]

Again, what aren't we worrying about that we need to be worrying about? What have our discussions failed to give proper weight to? Do we have corporate responsibilities that transcend the crush and crunch of the moment? Do we have the right to mess up a perfectly good cornfield?

In each of these cases, the board chairman in question had previously served as the CEO of his company. Each understood, from personal experience, how easy it is for even the brightest, most broad-gauged leadership team to get sucked into the press of the moment—and maybe, from some larger perspective, to drop the ball in the process. Each understood how important it is for the board to be willing and able to challenge the CEO and other corporate leaders, whether or not that is a comfortable experience.

Jay Lorsch, a Harvard Business School professor who has spent many years studying corporate boards, argued in 1989 that boards were originally intended to be "potentates," but over the years they had gradually degenerated into mere pawns of management.[5] Lorsch now maintains that many boards improved their performance dramatically in the decade of the 1990s.[6] The first two boards we're about to look at argue strongly against that conclusion.

FAST TIMES AT WORLDCOM

Everybody has some sense of how bad WorldCom was, but not many people understand how bad it really was. WorldCom was the invention of an eccentric character in Mississippi named Bernard "Bernie" Ebbers. Before becoming a telecom tycoon, Ebbers was a milkman, a bouncer, a high-school basketball coach, and the manager of a motel chain. Along with a few local cronies, Ebbers figured out a way to take advantage of the federal deregulation of the telephone industry—remember deregulation, in chapter 3?—and put together a sprawling empire by buying up regional long-distance companies in the 1980s and 1990s.[7]

Along the way, Ebbers also acquired board members. By the year 2000, almost all of WorldCom's directors were individuals who had headed the companies that WorldCom had purchased. Three problems, already: First, these individuals weren't particularly broad-gauged people. Second, they were all indebted to Ebbers, who had made them rich. Third, much of their wealth was tied up in WorldCom stock, which isn't a good formula for independent thinking. (By 2002, eight of the fifteen directors each owned more than a million shares in the company.)

At the turn of the century, WorldCom began to get into deep trouble. It's a complicated story; suffice it to say, however, that Wall Street expected WorldCom's dazzling year-over-year revenue growth of the 1990s to continue forever, but because of market conditions, that was an unrealistic expectation. Ebbers and his cronies therefore engaged in a series of accounting tricks to *simulate* a healthy company, including spending down earmarked reserves in contrary and inappropriate ways and—when they ran out of reserves—capitalizing expenses that were clearly operating costs of doing business. This had the effect of moving these costs from the company's income statements to its balance sheet, which "improved" pretax income—to the tune of some $3.8 billion in 2001 and 2002—and this made Wall Street happy.

In part to conceal these shenanigans, and in part because he believed in the power of secrecy, Ebbers (aided by his CFO, Scott Sullivan) effectively walled off most of the world from the company's true results. Even his board was kept in the dark. He told his directors almost nothing, and he prevented them from having meaningful contact with other than a few carefully selected (and complicit) corporate officers. He carefully scripted and dominated all board meetings. Up until the time they fired him in April 2002, the board had never met without Ebbers present.

Serving on WorldCom's board wasn't a particularly well-paying job. Each director received an annual retainer of $35,000 and an extra thousand dollars for each board meeting he or she attended. In addition, members of the compensation and audit committees got nominal additional compensation for meetings attended. Some have argued that the directors' relatively modest compensation contributed to their mail-it-in approach to their jobs, the degree of which in retrospect was astounding.

The three-person compensation committee at least had the decency to meet more or less regularly, even if they only "met" on the phone. And unfortunately, that's about the best you can say about them. Between January 1999 and December 2001, they lavished more than $77 million in various kinds of compensation on Ebbers. At the same time, Ebbers was running an interesting stable of outside businesses, including a rice farm in Louisiana, a lumber mill, a yacht building firm, a country club, a minor-league hockey team, and so on. Now, it was bad enough that Ebbers wasn't devoting most of his attention to WorldCom, but in addition, he persuaded the compensation committee to loan him huge sums of money to bail him out when his multiple outside businesses went bad.

Meanwhile, the chairman of the compensation committee accepted an offer from Ebbers to lease a WorldCom jet at well below market rates—and then failed to report the deal to his fellow board members for several months. Again, not a reflection of, or a prescription for, independent thinking!

WorldCom's audit committee performed even worse. They didn't meet very often—between three and five times a year—and tended to confer for only about an hour when they did get together. Remember that we're talking about a huge enterprise here, with lots of nooks and crannies, in a fast-changing industry, stapled together in a hurry over the previous decade or two. The audit committee, the board's primary watchdog, was asleep at its post. In addition, none of the four members of that committee had any significant financial expertise. So it's not surprising that no one on the audit committee ever had any inkling that something north of $9 *billion* of false or unsupported accounting entries had been passed through to them for rubber-stamping.

Arthur Andersen, WorldCom's outside auditors, also came up short. Yes, they were frustrated at every turn by WorldCom's strong tendencies toward compartmentalization and secrecy, but they didn't bother to complain to the audit committee that they weren't getting what they needed to do their job. (And yes, that was

Andersen's obligation.) In June 2001, Andersen's accountants held an internal brainstorming session to run scenarios as to how WorldCom might hoodwink Andersen—and by extension, the investment community—should Ebbers and his gang ever choose to do so. One of the scenarios they ran involved the inappropriate capitalization of costs. But Andersen, deciding that it wasn't likely, simply discarded the scenario.

The result? One of the largest public company accounting frauds in history. We heard a lot about Enron in this same time period. (In fact, by unhappy coincidence, WorldCom fired Andersen as its accountant when Andersen got into trouble at Enron.) But WorldCom's bankruptcy, filed in the summer of 2002, was twice as big as Enron's (December 2001) and four times as big as that of the notorious Global Crossing (January 2002). And yes, we should lay the WorldCom disaster at the feet of Ebbers and Sullivan. But as I noted earlier, there's the boss, and then there's the boss's boss. At WorldCom, the boss's boss—the board—also dropped the ball.

Or more accurately, they never even bothered to pick it up.

ENRON: EVEN WORSE THAN WORLDCOM?

When it comes to Enron, the first challenging question is, *Where to start?*[8]

Enron has become the most notorious entity in corporate America. That's too bad, in a sense. Almost all of the 20,000 people who worked for Enron deserved better. There was a time when Enron was just a humble old-line energy company, with power plants and pipelines, moving things from here to there in a sturdy sort of way. Then it got hijacked by finance hotshots, ensnared by the McKinsey philosophy of asset-light corporate buccaneering, and let down in a deadly way by its board.

Again, our focus here is the board. Here's how the Senate investigators assessed their performance:

The Enron Board of Directors failed to safeguard Enron shareholders and contributed to the collapse of the seventh largest public company in the United States, by allowing Enron to engage in high risk accounting, inappropriate conflict of interest transactions, extensive undisclosed off-the-books activities, and excessive executive compensation. The Board witnessed numerous indications of questionable practices by Enron management over the years, but chose to ignore them to the detriment of Enron shareholders, employees and business associates.

Let's get a little background on the table, so we can understand these board failures in context.

Enron in the 1990s made a transition: from the sleepy company described above to a snap-crackle-pop enterprise that specialized in the virtual. Instead of pushing things through pipelines, Enron began to specialize in buying and selling energy contracts online. With a little help from its friends in Washington, as described in chapter 3, Enron got the authority to start treating these contracts as marketable commodities—but commodities that weren't subject to the kinds of restrictions that the SEC and the stock exchanges imposed on "normal" commodities.

Well, when this scheme was good, it was very good, at least on paper, and when it was bad, it stank. First of all, Enron now had to get its hands on huge pools of capital so that it could meet its contractual obligations at the end of each online trading day. In addition, by its very nature, this was a lumpy sort of business, with extreme quarterly fluctuations. Because such a fluctuation could drive up Enron's cost of borrowing—and thus drive down profitability—the company had all kinds of incentives to smooth out its earnings, quarter to quarter. Just as WorldCom had to show enough growth year-over-year to retain the affection of fickle Wall Street, Enron had to present a pleasant quarter-to-quarter picture to hard-nosed Moody's and Standard & Poor's, the all-important credit-rating agencies.

So if you're Enron, how do you do that? Well, you can develop specialized contracts involving prepayment for energy over multiple years, and then you can hedge and pool and otherwise play games with these contracts to a fare-thee-well. (*Let the regulators try to figure out* that *stuff!*) And you can either milk or dump your assets, as you make the transition from a traditional company to an "asset-light" enterprise. If you can't sell the asset, you can syndicate it—that is, sell it off to groups of buyers who are willing to take a piece of the action—and call the proceeds from these syndications "earnings."

If you look back to the WorldCom story and compare it to Enron's, you can start to see a pattern. When these companies don't generate the anticipated (and needed) earnings, they pull out the books and start relabeling stuff. There's not an accountant in the world—except maybe in the Houston office of Arthur Anderson, circa 2000—who would buy the argument that "selling off an asset" equals "dollars earned." And yet, there was Enron, fooling the world and getting away with it.

In truth, not everybody was fooled, and this in turn created new problems. What do you do when you can't find enough people foolish enough to invest in these shaky syndications? Easy—you invent your own buyers! And that's what Enron did next. The company set up what it called "unconsolidated affiliates" to which it would sell or syndicate its assets. What's an unconsolidated affiliate? Good question. It's kind of like a blood relative who—according to you—is no relation to you, unless of course on a given day it's useful for you to claim that relationship.

So Enron set up a series of entities that were not included in the parent company's financial statements—to avoid accusations of self-dealing—but whose assets it claimed when it was convenient to do so. In October 2000, for example, Enron's managers told the board that the company had a total of $60 billion in assets. Sounds like a lot—unless you take away the assets of the unconsolidated affiliates, which accounted for some $27 billion of that total. Here today, gone tomorrow, but back again on Thursday (if needed).

The names of these so-called partnerships—names like Whitewing, LJM, JEDI, Raptor, and the Hawaii 125-0 Trust—have long since entered the Business Hall of Shame. But the real bad guys in this sorry tale, obviously, were the Enron finance hotshots who dreamed all this stuff up in the first place. To make a long story short, the self-dealing at the corporate level allegedly came down to the personal level, as well—including (according to the Justice Department's indictment) securities fraud, insider trading, falsification of accounting records, and—again—self-dealing.[9] Members of Enron's senior management allegedly skimmed off millions of dollars in inappropriate deals, to the detriment of Enron shareholders. In one notable example, CFO Fastow invested $25,000 in a partnership and two months later received—through a family foundation—a return of $4.5 million!

In the way of settlement, while they denied any wrongdoing, ten Enron board members and ten WorldCom board members all recently agreed to personal payments of restitution, with the WorldCom directors paying more—relative to their personal net worth—than the Enron directors. It should have been the other way around. Enron's board should have been held to a higher standard than WorldCom's. Unlike WorldCom's board, this wasn't a bunch of good old boys who lucked out and found themselves in the telecommunications fast lane. Enron's directors were a worldly bunch who were fully up to the task of figuring out what their company was doing. One Enron director—Dr. Robert Jaedicke, who was chair of the audit committee—was a former faculty member and former dean at the Stanford Business School with a world-renowned expertise in managerial accounting. Jaedicke "wrote the book," as they say.

I've already quoted the Senate subcommittee's opinion of the Enron board's fiduciary failure. Here's the rest of the subcommittee's scathing assessment of that board:

> **High risk accounting.** The Enron Board of Directors knowingly allowed Enron to engage in high risk accounting practices.
>
> **Inappropriate conflicts of interest.** Despite clear conflicts of interest, the Enron Board of Directors approved an unprecedented arrangement allowing Enron's Chief Financial Officer to establish and operate . . . private equity funds which transacted business with Enron and profited at Enron's expense. The Board exercised inadequate oversight of [these funds'] transaction and compensation controls, and failed to protect Enron shareholders from unfair dealing.

Extensive undisclosed off-the-books activity. The Enron Board of Directors knowingly allowed Enron to conduct billions of dollars in off-the-books activity to make its financial condition appear better than it was and failed to ensure adequate public disclosure of material off-the-books liabilities that contributed to Enron's collapse.

Excessive compensation. The Enron Board of Directors approved excessive compensation for company executives, failed to monitor the cumulative cash drain caused by Enron's 2000 annual bonus and performance unit plans, and failed to monitor or halt abuse by Board Chairman and Chief Executive Officer Kenneth Lay of a company-financed, multi-million dollar, personal credit line.

Lack of independence. The independence of the Enron Board of Directors was compromised by financial ties between the company and certain Board members. The Board also failed to ensure the independence of the company's auditor, allowing Andersen to provide internal audit and consulting services while serving as Enron's outside auditor.

Enron's board was organized into five committees. The *executive committee* handled urgent business matters between board meetings. The *finance committee* reviewed major proposed financial transactions. The *audit and compliance committee*—chaired by Jaedicke—reviewed the company's financial statements (based on information supplied by the company and work performed by Andersen) and was supposed to ensure that the company complied with relevant regulations. Five of the six members of this committee had significant training and experience in managerial accounting. The *compensation committee* was responsible for setting and monitoring compensation policies for the company's senior managers, and the *nominating committee* picked candidates for board membership.

Although the Enron board and its committees seem to have punched the clock a little more regularly than their counterparts at WorldCom, some of the same structural problems were in evidence at both companies. "Board members appeared to have routine contact with less than a dozen senior officers at Enron," noted the Senate investigators. "The Board did not have a practice of meeting without Enron management present." Enron board members had almost no contact with one another, or with members of the management team, between the formal board meetings.

Where the resemblances to WorldCom stop, however, the Enron directors start to look much worse—all the more so because they were skilled and experienced enough to know better. Materials obtained by the Senate investigators suggest that, unlike at WorldCom, Arthur Andersen knew full well that Enron was on shaky ground and effectively conveyed that opinion to the audit committee. In February 1999, for example, Andersen told the audit committee that Enron was using accounting practices that "push[ed] limits," or were "at the edge" of acceptable practice. The audit committee did nothing in response. By failing to act, it gave its tacit approval to these practices.

The compensation committee looks no better. Like their counterparts at WorldCom, Enron's directors were incredibly generous to the company's managers—not only awarding them outlandish pay and bonuses, but using corporate assets to bail out wayward executives. For example, the compensation committee set up a $4 million personal line of credit for Ken Lay; when this proved inadequate, they raised the limit to $7.5 million. As it later turned out, Lay got in the habit of drawing down the entire amount available and then "paying it back" in shares of Enron stock. In a single year—between October 2000 and October 2001—Lay took *$77 million* in cash out of the company and handed over artificially pumped-up Enron shares in return. The compensation committee failed to monitor Lay's use of this personal piggy bank.

Meanwhile, the compensation committee had no particular idea of exactly how generous it was being toward the larger management team. It approved annual and special bonus plans and then paid no attention to what those plans cost the company. In early 2001, for example, Enron paid out almost $750 million in cash bonuses—in a year when the company's entire net income was

$975 million. According to Senate investigators, no one on the compensation committee ever sat down and figured this out.

Perhaps most shocking, in all this, is the complete lack of guilt, shame, remorse, or even ambivalence shown by the Enron board in the wake of the company's horrific unraveling. The seventh-largest publicly held company in the United States wound up a smoking, shattered hulk. To a man (and a woman), Enron's directors claimed that they had done their jobs as well as could be expected under the circumstances. "Unfortunately," said interim board chairman Norman Blake, testifying before Congress, "I believe that we were uninformed because management and outside experts who reported to us failed to do their jobs and give us full complete information."[10]

Audit committee chair Jaedicke, in his testimony, added a little twist. He said that his group had done about as well as could be expected under *any* circumstances:

> We do not work full time in this job. None of the members of the Audit Committee is an employee of Enron. We do not manage the Company. We do not do the auditing. We are not detectives. . . .
>
> We were entitled to rely on the representations made to us about the appropriateness of the accounting for the partnerships, and the adequacy of disclosure. We asked questions. We provided oversight, and set direction based on the information we received. I respectfully submit that we did our job.[11]

Blake, Jaedicke, and their fellow directors could and should have done a whole lot better. Becoming the member of the board of a company like Enron, circa 1999, was a little like getting in the passenger seat of a Porsche Turbo: you *know* it goes fast. Knowing that, you keep an eye on the driver. If the driver starts taking the turns too fast, you tap him on the shoulder and make him slow down. If you don't, and the cops later pull you over, don't say you didn't see the scenery whizzing by. You did.

And incidentally, you enjoyed the ride. Blake realized $1.7 million on his sale of 21,200 shares of Enron stock, and Jaedicke realized $840,000 on his sale of just over 13,000 shares.[12] There are a lot of people who sold later—or who never got the chance to sell—who didn't enjoy their rides anywhere near as much.

THE ANTIDOTE: THE GENERAL ELECTRIC APPROACH

So where does that leave us? Wringing our hands and crying in our beer? Concluding that being a director is too tough and that our expectations for a board member are unrealistically high?

Absolutely not. And for evidence, we should look to the board of directors of General Electric. First things first: GE works its directors pretty hard. In 2002, for example, they held thirteen scheduled meetings. (Contrast this with the WorldCom board, which met between four and six times a year.) At GE, moreover, directors are expected to show up: attendance at these and scheduled committee meetings was more than 92 percent.[13] Board members are strongly discouraged from serving on more than one other "major" board, because a GE directorship is considered heavy lifting.

And GE's directors are very well paid for that heavy lifting. Up through 2002, they each received an annual retainer of $75,000, meeting fees of $2,000 per meeting, and 18,000 stock options (worth something like $168,000). In 2003, this system was simplified, and directors now receive a combination of cash and deferred stock units totaling $250,000—in other words, the same level of pay, but structured differently.[14] So four years on GE's board is worth a million bucks, as well as a lot of other nice perks and bennies—contributions to your favorite charity, life insurance, and so on.

Again, contrast this with the WorldCom setup, where directors were paid less than half as much and received significantly less generous options and "goodies" packages. Where do you think the better talent will migrate? Where do you think directors will work harder and be more conscientious?

A review of GE's governance principles yields some additional useful tips.[15] The corporation has decided that a majority of directors need to be "independent," and it has carefully defined what that term means. (As of 2003, eleven of GE's sixteen directors qualified as independent, according to guidelines that match or are tougher than those of the New York Stock Exchange.) Committees circulate notes of their meetings to the full board as soon as they are available. Nonemployee directors are required to have at least three regularly scheduled meetings per year without management present. Committees are required to perform an annual self-evaluation. The head of the management development and compensation committee is identified as the "presiding director"—often called a "lead director" in other settings—and he or she serves as an important counterbalance (and complement) to the CEO.

"The board shall be responsible for its agenda," according to the governance principles—a sharp contrast to both WorldCom and Enron. At the December board meeting, the CEO and the presiding director work with the full board to rough out an agenda for the following year's meetings; in advance of each subsequent meeting, the presiding director reviews the CEO's proposed agenda for the meeting and either approves or rejects it. "Directors are urged to make suggestions for agenda items, or additional premeeting materials, to the CEO, the presiding director, or appropriate committee chair at any time."

Here's a governance principle that's compelling, in part because it's so clear and so clearly right: "GE will not make any personal loans or extensions of credit to directors or executive officers, other than consumer loans for credit card services on terms offered to the general public." Remember Bernie Ebbers, back at WorldCom? Before the ax came down, his board loaned him something like $400 million in shareholders' money. True, these kinds of loans are now forbidden by the feds, but it's still nice to see it in black and white. *Thou shalt not!*

Here's an interesting GE *thou shalt,* probably inspired by the horror stories coming out of WorldCom and Enron: "Nonemployee directors are encouraged to contact senior managers of the company without senior corporate management present. To facilitate such contact, non-employee directors are expected to make two regularly scheduled visits to GE businesses a year without corporate management being present." Take it from me: there is no CEO in the country, not even GE's exceptional Jeff Immelt, who can install obfuscating smoke and mirrors at thirty-two sites a year (sixteen directors times two sites each). Those traveling directors are bound to see some version of reality.

I'd be the last to say that GE is perfect or that its board hasn't made an occasional mistake. And it's clear that GE has sometimes been pushed from behind by good-governance advocates within its shareholder base, rather than motivated by the desire to do the right thing.

Nevertheless, GE is clearly getting there. In February 2004, Governance Metrics International, a self-described "corporate governance research and ratings agency," announced its new ratings on 2,100 companies around the world. GE was one of only eighteen companies in the United States—and one of only twenty-two in the world—to score a perfect ten.[16]

Companies elsewhere in the world may have a harder time scoring a ten. In many countries around the world, legislation and regulations don't necessarily push in the right (and same) direction. But there's no reason at all why a lot more U.S. companies can't hit a similar standard. They just have to *want* to.

This is a book about CEOs and their responsibilities. But it doesn't take only a CEO to get it right. A CEO coming from the right ethical direction, with a great board behind him or her, has it a whole lot easier than one who is trying to swim the channel unassisted.

7

OUTSOURCING AND OFFSHORING

So there's these two angels standing on a cloud, just inside the pearly gates. One of them—who has a real nice pair of wings on his back—is fitting out the other one with what appears to be his very first set of wings. The equipment-manager angel is standing in front of a cardboard carton that has a bunch of wings sticking out of it.

"We design them here," he says, "but the labor is cheaper in Hell." (Apologies to *The New Yorker,* where the cartoon originally ran.)[1]

The New Yorker has also taken a far more serious look at the same topic—the decidedly unfunny outsourcing and offshoring of American jobs. In March 2004, the magazine printed a nonfiction account of life in Cameron County, Texas, in the wake of the closing of the local Fruit of the Loom factory.[2] The article documents the travails of a local family, the Sanchezes, who want nothing more than to live the American Dream—in which they believe 100 percent—but who are being beaten up, time and time again, by the disappearance of manufacturing jobs from south Texas. They *want* to play by the rules, but the rules keep changing, and always to their disadvantage.

At first, as you're reading about the Sanchezes and south Texas, this seems to be a NAFTA-offshoring story—a story about the flight of jobs out of the United States (in this case, the Brownsville area) to nearby Mexico. But as you read on, you learn that Mexico too is hemorrhaging jobs. The benefits of the preferred status afforded to Mexico by NAFTA in 1994 were short-lived, as the United States subsequently signed new pacts with China and other trading partners. Mexico quickly lost jobs to Honduras, and Honduras lost jobs to China. And not just a few jobs. "In just three years," according to *The New Yorker,* "a quarter of a million Mexican manufacturing jobs had disappeared. Among those jobs were several thousand at Mexico-based Fruit of the Loom factories."[3]

OFFSHORING OUR UNDERWEAR

Fruit of the Loom? Why does that name sound so familiar?

Well, aside from owning the brand name that many of us privately encounter several times a day, this once-proud company has been a regular newsmaker over the past decade or so. In the mid-1990s, FTL's stock started heating up. At that time, Wall Street loved CEO William F. Farley, who admired himself enough to 1) model FTL underwear in TV ads and 2) tout himself as presidential (*U.S.* presidential) material. Wall Street also loved FTL's aggressive policy of offshoring: cutting jobs in high-wage areas (read "the United States") and replacing them with jobs in less-expensive labor markets (read "almost anywhere else"). According to a lawsuit later filed by the Service Employees International Union, FTL under Farley moved some 16,000 U.S. jobs offshore.[4] The stock soared to $44. Life was good, at least for senior management and shareholders.

Then came the 1998 class-action lawsuit that charged Farley and other senior FTL managers with insider trading by artificially inflating the price of FTL's stock and rapidly unloading their stock just before news of the company's wretched operating results for the first half of 1997 became public.[5] Next came revelations that Farley's own private company had billed something like $100 million in management fees to FTL—legal, but odoriferous. (And yes, that was in addition to the $40 million or so in stock options, salary, and bonuses that Farley took home in the mid-1990s.) Then came FTL's relocation of its headquarters to the Cayman Islands to reduce its tax bill. Then revelations about $65 million in personal loan guarantees to Farley by the company. (Again, all perfectly legal, but not something you want a whole lot of publicity about.) Then Farley's firing by the FTL board in August 1999. Then, only four months later, bankruptcy. Wall Street's former darling had managed to lose $576 million in a single year.[6] The stock price plummeted to near-invisibility.

The company started slashing costs—mainly by cutting jobs and, yes, moving even more jobs offshore. FTL's job base in its home state of Kentucky dwindled to 1,200 (down from 9,000 a decade earlier).[7] The company closed its yarn mill in Jacksonville, Alabama (a cost-cutting move that actually hurt the company's numbers, at least in the short term, by incurring consolidation costs).[8] At the same time, FTL started whittling away at its manufacturing facilities in the Irish cities of Donegal and Derry in favor of a factory outside Rabat, Morocco. There, according to the Brussels-based International Textile, Garment and Leather Workers' Federation (ITGLWF), the company proceeded to engage in heavy-handed union-busting tactics. Commented one union leader,

> Fruit of the Loom has long abused workers rights in its US plants. Then the job losses in Derry and Donegal were a devastating blow to the local economy. Now it is workers in Morocco who are feeling the brunt of the company's disgraceful behavior. Of course, these workers need the jobs, but unless they have the right to organize and bargain collectively for decent wages and working conditions, neither the workers nor their communities will benefit.[9]

From bad to worse, right? Yes, but not to worry! Even at this darkest moment in the company's increasingly troubled history, a white knight was riding into view on the horizon. In late 2001, Berkshire Hathaway announced that it had cut a deal to acquire FTL for $835 million in cash. Warren Buffett, legendary investor and chairman of Berkshire Hathaway, announced that he liked the "strength of the [FTL] brand" and the "managerial talent of John Holland."[10]

It's worth underscoring that although Buffett liked the manage-rial talent of COO Holland—who had been brought out of retire-ment to help save the beleaguered company—he had nothing to say about the disgraced and departed William F. Farley. Buffett's si-lence on the subject of Farley is certainly understandable, because Farley was an ongoing embarrassment. In the wake of scooping up all the goodies described above, running FTL into the ground, and getting bounced out on his ear, Farley made loud noises about how he was owed *another* $100 million in unpaid severance and pen-sion benefits—and even threatened legal action to get what he claimed he was owed.[11]

Don't you love a guy with chutzpah? It takes a CEO—in the worst sense of the phrase.

So Warren Buffett arrived on the scene—an unexpected turn of events that "sparked applause on the Cameron County [Texas] shop floor," according to *The New Yorker*.[12] People evidently as-sumed that a smart guy like Buffett would save their jobs. As it turned out, that assumption was wrong. At the end of 2003, less than a year and a half after its acquisition by Berkshire Hathaway, FTL completed the shutdown of its Cameron County facility, throwing the last eight hundred people out of work. A year later, it closed its last Irish facilities, again in favor of Morocco.[13]

One thing to keep in mind here is that Berkshire Hathaway's profits doubled in 2003, the same year that the Texas plant was closed. That's right: profits doubled over 2002, which Buffett—in the company's 2002 annual report—had already celebrated as a "banner year." So 2003 must have been a double-banner year.

It's also interesting to note that in his letter sent with the company's 2003 annual report, Buffett (the earth's second-wealthiest inhabitant) blasted the directors of mutual funds for not taking better care of the interests of their shareholders:

I am on my soapbox now only because the blatant wrongdoing that has occurred has betrayed the trust of so many millions of shareholders. Hundreds of industry insiders had to know what was going on, yet none publicly said a word. It took Eliot Spitzer, and the whistleblowers who aided him, to initiate a housecleaning. We urge fund directors to continue the job. Like directors throughout Corporate America, these fiduciaries must now decide whether their job is to work for owners or for managers.[14]

Warren Buffett has certainly earned his soapbox, even if he trots it out at strange moments. (One such moment was when he turned up as an adviser to Arnold Schwarzenegger during that actor's successful effort to unseat California's sitting governor.) And sometimes it's a breath of fresh air that emanates from Buffett's hometown of Omaha. In fact, I agree with his basic premise that mutual-fund directors have to mind the store better and look out for the interests of their shareholders.

But the conduct of Fruit of the Loom, especially as carried forward by new owner Berkshire Hathaway, demands a broadening of the debate. As long as we talk *only* about the needs of shareholders—as long as we focus on delivering goodies to only one of the legitimate stakeholders in a business and proudly wave our double banners in the air—we're walking down an immoral and dangerous path.

NOT ONE BUT FIVE STAKEHOLDERS

It's painful to have to include a section with this title. For a CEO who is an ethical person—and most of them are—it should be perfectly obvious that there are at least five stakeholders to worry about. But apparently, it isn't all that obvious.

My arrival at the Standford Business School in the fall of 1969 happened to coincide with what turned out to be a relatively brief flurry of interest, both in academia and in business, in something called corporate social responsibility (CSR). I remember reading and hearing about how corporations had started out centuries earlier as creatures in service only to their owners, and how—over difficult decades and centuries, and as the result of cumulative legal and regulatory pressures—they gradually had acquired broader responsibilities. It was no longer enough (I learned) to turn the biggest possible buck for your shareholders. As a responsible corporate citizen, you had to think about a bigger picture.[15]

Slowly, very slowly, especially in the Progressive Era and subsequently, corporations were compelled to take responsibility for that river that they had always taken for granted. (Before that it was *We dump those nasty effluents into that body of moving water that just happens to be conveniently located beneath our factory, and hey, they disappear!*) Similarly, corporations were required to take into account their impact on the communities around them. And finally, they were obliged to take better care of their workers.

Or, to phrase it a little more generously, they were finally *allowed* to do so. Before the courts and the regulators intervened on the side of CSR, managers had to worry that they might be fired by their stockholders if they tried to use corporate funds to clean up a river or otherwise act as "do-gooders." It wasn't until some favorable IRS rulings in the late 1940s, for example, that corporations could legally spend pretax dollars in philanthropic directions.

In studying this history, I came to realize that corporations had five stakeholders: shareholders—sure, we can put them first—employees, customers, community, and industry. The essence of CSR was to hold a proposed corporate action up to the stakeholders lens and see whether anybody would be unduly harmed by that action. My experience was typical of that day. Most business-school students—as well as most corporate moguls—were hearing the same things and reaching more or less the same conclusions.

I carried this perspective into my first job, as Ed Littlefield's assistant at Utah International. After two years in that role, I went to work as general manager of the Navajo Mine, then the world's largest coal mine, which is located on the Navajo Reservation in the Four Corners area of northwest New Mexico. Yes, we had our share of critics in the environmental community. (You may even have seen one of those debates on *60 Minutes*.) But I can honestly say that we tried to use that CSR stakeholders lens each and every day, and especially when we faced tough decisions. For example, because the Navajo Mine was located on the Navajo Reservation and about 75 percent of our workforce were Navajos, we were sensitive to issues of reclamation, senior manager diversity, alcoholism programs, and—for the first time ever on the reservation—well-baby care. So community was one touchstone of CSR that we had in the front of our minds, all the time.

Again, I don't think my management team and my company were unique in this regard. Lots of companies believed in figuring out the right thing to do and then doing it. Hollywood made exciting movies about the notable exceptions to this rule—*Silkwood, Norma Rae, The China Syndrome,* and so on—but most of the rest of us plodded along in the best manner we could.

Then, somewhere in the mid-seventies and continuing into the eighties, there was a quiet revolution—a rebellion that looked significant at the time but that looks *enormous* in retrospect. Let's date the beginning of the revolution, arbitrarily, to September 13, 1970. That was the day when the *New York Times* published an article by a then relatively obscure University of Chicago economist named Milton Friedman. The article had a succinct headline: "The Social Responsibility of Business Is to Increase Its Profits."

That article wasn't particularly in step with the times, and it wasn't much related to the work that won Friedman a Nobel Prize in 1976. (That work involved the relationship between the money supply and prices, work that ultimately served as an underpinning for what became Reaganomics.) But the article spawned a whole cottage industry of conservative academic imitators, who began undermining the basic tenets of CSR.

Friedman and his imitators also helped unleash upon the world an onslaught of opportunists in business, who collectively became known as "corporate raiders" by their detractors. T. Boone Pickens—who attempted takeovers of Cities Service and Gulf Oil, among other companies—is probably the most notorious of these guys, but there were lots of others. Basically, their tactic was to persuade a majority of shareholders in a company that management wasn't looking after their interests—à la the mutual-fund directors that Buffett later scolded—and that they should go along with a hostile takeover of the company. In the wake of the takeover, they promised, a sleek new management team would create a lean, mean, and hungry corporation, focused on delivering higher returns to investors.

In light of today's stratospheric executive salaries, it's ironic to remember that one of the arguments of the corporate raiders was that CEOs and other senior executives were overpaid. *Fat, dumb, and happy,* said the raiders of the corporate establishment. *Off with their overpaid, complacent heads!*

Certainly, lots of other things were going on at this same time that compounded the problem. American manufacturers were waking up to the fact that they were not particularly competitive in the world marketplace, either in terms of cost or quality. The Japanese carmakers that Detroit used to sneer at began eating Detroit's lunch. In the early 1980s, the Japanese upstarts could land a car on American soil that cost something like $1,500 less than a comparably equipped American car, and the Japanese car also worked better and lasted longer—not a strong competitive position for GM, Ford, and Chrysler! The artificial energy crises of the 1970s, as well as the wicked recession of the early Reagan years, also contributed to a general sense of insecurity.

So all these factors converged at the same point: U.S. corporations had to do something different. And one thing they decided to do was to stop acting like good corporate citizens. *Hey*—the argument went—*when the barn's on fire, you don't worry about the farmhands!*

Consider this unhealthy trend: in 1981, the Business Roundtable—an organization of CEOs intended to look after the interests of business in the public-policy arena—officially endorsed a policy that said that shareholder returns had to be balanced against other considerations. In other words, they endorsed the core premise of CSR. But in 1997, that same Business Roundtable concluded that the job of business was to maximize shareholder wealth.[16]

So there you have it: nearly a century of progress along the path of persuading corporations to act responsibly, and then a near-complete reversal of gears in less than two decades. By the time Bill Farley started driving Fruit of the Loom into the ground, nobody was even asking CSR-like questions anymore. Who cares what's good for Cameron County, or Derry, Ireland, or Rabat, Morocco? Who cares what's good for the company's employees? That's not the point.

The point, apparently, is to maximize shareholder wealth, and *there is no other point.* Allocative efficiency in the marketplace! Let capital flow where it is most effectively deployed, let a few crumbs fall off the tables of the wealthy, and the devil take the hindmost! Anyone who raises an ethical or philosophical objection to this approach is dismissed not just as a hand-wringing liberal, but as an *outdated* hand-wringing liberal.

But wait a minute. One could easily make the case that shareholders are already a disproportionately privileged class. So, faced with a distributive social-policy choice, why favor their interests over those of rank-and-file employees, who generally are not a privileged class?[17] Because shareholders are "owners"? What about the fact that the average length of stock ownership in this country has declined precipitously—from over ten years in the early 1960s to under six months today? We're not talking long-term Andrew Carnegie–type owners, here; we're talking about people who scoot around quarter to quarter looking for the best short-term returns, most often through financial intermediaries like mutual funds.

In light of this fact, who's got the more legitimate claim on that now-shuttered factory in Cameron County—the eight hundred people who used to work there, or Warren Buffett's shareholders? Before you answer that question: you do know that a single share of Berkshire Hathaway costs north of $90,000, right? Buffett doesn't believe in stock splits.

Cup your hand to your ear, and listen for the chorus: *Outdated hand-wringing, bleeding-heart liberal chump! Get with the program!*

YOU AIN'T SEEN NOTHIN' YET

In an op-ed piece in a recent issue of *BusinessWeek*, Jeffrey E. Garten, dean of the Yale School of Management, weighed in on the subject of offshoring.[18] Garten began his editorial—provocatively titled "Offshoring: You Ain't Seen Nothin' Yet!"—by pointing out that so far the United States has lost "only" between 1 million and 2 million jobs to offshoring, and that this is a relatively small number when compared with an overall base of 140 million American jobs.

However, Garten went on to point out, another 5 million to 10 million jobs will likely be moving offshore in the next five to ten years. (Does "10 percent of all jobs in America" get your attention?) Moreover, Garten continued, the increasing mobility of jobs in the global marketplace will certainly exert downward pressure on wages paid to the remaining workers in the United States. It's not just how many jobs are left; it's also what's left of the jobs that are left. Workers will be forced into simply holding on to what they've got—or agreeing to givebacks and diminished benefits.

And it's not just manufacturing jobs that are at risk. In recent years, we've seen the phenomenon of so-called higher-skilled jobs leaving town—first in the back offices of financial services firms and more recently in the middle-professional ranks of high-tech firms. "We didn't anticipate how quickly this transformation would occur," said Deloitte & Touche's director of research in June 2004, reporting on a study that his consulting firm had just completed.[19] He was referring to the fact that in 2002, the percentage of global financial services firms with an offshore capacity was 29 percent; only a year later, it was *67 percent.*

Interestingly enough, the Deloitte study pointed out that offshoring was increasingly happening at the expense of outsourcing. (In other words, rather than buying back-office services from a freestanding American firm down the street or out in windswept South Dakota, the global financial-services giants now prefer to "build their own" offshore.) What does that sound like to you? Sounds like even more jobs moving offshore, right? And as the final insult, the Deloitte study concluded that even though there had been a spate of negative publicity about offshoring in recent months, "most companies interviewed did not think this would have a significant impact in the long term." No, the companies aren't saying that offshoring wouldn't have a significant impact—only that negative publicity about offshoring doesn't worry them too much.

But Americans are still king when it comes to the good jobs, right? Like high-end software engineering? Well, maybe not. Beginning in 2001, according to the *New York Times,* Microsoft began hiring Indian software architects to do relatively high-level design work.[20] Curiously, much of this work is done by Indians whom Microsoft flies to the United States and who work here on special H-1B visas. This is the onshore version of offshoring, apparently. But this just makes my case even more forcefully. Microsoft can pay these guys an annualized rate of $180,000—less than a quarter of which goes to the engineers themselves, by the way; the rest goes to their Indian employers—fly them to and from India coach class, and still do better than it would hiring their U.S. counterparts.

And did you hear about IBM's plans to move up to 4,730 skilled jobs to India and China? Let's make that a little less abstract. These are jobs that (according to internal IBM documents) pay between $75,000 and $100,000 a year. That's something like $400 million in middle-class payrolls that will leave Southbury, Connecticut; Poughkeepsie, New York; Raleigh, North Carolina; Dallas, Texas; and Boulder, Colorado, among other places.[21] Know anybody there who owns a house or thought their children might end up working locally for IBM?

How about radiologists? *They've* got nothing to worry about, right? It takes a lot of skill to read an X-ray, there must be lots of restrictive regulation, and anyway, the radiologist has to be somewhere in physical proximity to the patient, right?

Well, according to the *New York Times,* those top-of-the-food-chain radiologists might want to start keeping their resumes current. A skilled radiologist in the United States makes upwards of $250,000 a year. His or her counterpart in India makes $25,000. A doctor at Boston's Massachusetts General Hospital recently came up with a scheme to send X-rays as electronic files to a company in India, where they are subjected to a preliminary read and beamed back to this country. When word of this operation got out, radiologists across the United States howled. The American College of Radiology set up a task force to investigate the sacrilege. The radiologists' Web site (www.auntminnie.com) positively lit up with angry commentary.[22]

Now let's tie CEO compensation to offshoring. According to a study released by the Institute for Policy Studies in August 2004, the U.S. companies that outsourced the most jobs in 2003 also awarded well-above-average increases in compensation to their CEOs.[23] Unfortunately, the people who conducted the study didn't take the next logical step and say *why* that might be the case. But just to look at one scenario: wouldn't a CEO who hadn't already jumped on the offshoring bandwagon get motivated to do so if he or she came across the findings of this particular study? *Let me see: the more jobs I send overseas, the more I will benefit personally!*

Not convinced that you "ain't seen nothin' yet"? Well, consider a recent *Boston Globe* article that described how venture-capital companies in the Boston area are now insisting that high-tech start-ups include their offshoring plans in their initial business plan.[24] Given that Boston happens to be on the relatively conservative end of the venture-capital spectrum, I think it's safe to assume that the same thing is happening in the New York and Silicon Valley venture communities—only more so. So in the future, we're not going to see offshoring simply as an afterthought. It's going to be built in, from day one. The entrepreneur—who in the past has been an important generator of new jobs for Americans—is going to have to persuade his financial backers that he's moved just as many jobs as possible offshore. No credible plan for offshoring? Sorry! No start-up money.

No Easy Answers, but . . .

Outsourcing and offshoring were forecasted by most economists to be about the fair and reciprocal exchange between countries of labor-intensive jobs to recognize relative market and skills differentials. They were not intended as a way to promote child labor, abuse the global environment, and beat down domestic wages and benefits. They were not supposed to create a one-way flow: millions of jobs going out of the United States, none coming in.

To a certain extent, we're victims of our own past successes. One reason that the United States, more than most western countries, is losing service jobs to places like India is that English has emerged as the universal language of commerce and global education. You might call it the Revenge of the British Empire. But if the question is, *How many Finnish or German language call centers are getting set up in Bangalore?* the answer is zero.

This is serious business. If we continue to lose reasonably high-paying manufacturing and clerical jobs and replace them with low-paying service jobs, our economy (at the local, state, and national levels) must inevitably spiral downward. Perversely, health-care costs will inevitably go up, hitting the victims of this spiral with the second half of a double whammy: lower wages, higher costs.

Let's venture out on the thin ice of political incorrectness. Half of the people in this country have IQs above 100, and half have IQs below 100. (That's how IQs are supposed to work: 100 is the median.) We're hearing a lot of talk currently about how education is the solution to outsourcing and offshoring. But the fact is that a reasonably large and irreducible minimum of our population will never become radiologists—even if radiology were still a safe career bet. A certain number of people in our society want and need the opportunity to work in a factory, or in the back office of a financial services firm, or in the customer-service center of an airline. Maybe those displaced IBM-ers in Poughkeepsie can step sideways into another upper-middle-class job, but the point of the *New Yorker* story at the beginning of this chapter is that the Sanchezes, and people like them, really have no place else to go. Education alone isn't going to solve the problem, if a) you aren't cut out to be a computer technician, or b) there is no place to ply your new trade.

So what are we going to do about this mess?

Unfortunately, there are no easy answers. Capital does need to flow to where it can be deployed profitably. Capitalism does involve "creative destruction," as economist Joseph Schumpeter phrased it. When someone finds a better way to do something—and yes, a better place in which to do it—the old eventually has to give way to the new.

But we need a more careful and more complete calculation of where our *interests* and *responsibilities* lie. NPR recently ran a story about how the French government had decided to subsidize a private shipyard in order to keep it open. Some French bureaucrat somewhere sat down with a sharp pencil and figured out that if you took into account lost income taxes, increased unemployment payouts, increased health-care costs to the government, and so on, let-ting the shipyard go under would cost much more than the subsidy needed to keep it open. And this calculation didn't even touch upon issues like national security (Does the nation benefit from retaining the capacity to build and repair ships?) or personal pride (Is the na-tion better off having shipyard workers or idled people smoking Gauloises on street corners?). That bureaucrat in France appar-ently said, *We have an* interest *in keeping these people working, and we have a* responsibility *to make sure that they have a chance to do so.*

Cup your hand to your ear, and listen for the chorus: *Outdated hand-wringing, bleeding-heart liberal chump! Get with the pro-gram!*

Well, to hell with the chorus. We have to think bigger and do better. In particular there's a lot of work to be done in the policy-making realm. Economist Gene Sperling has laid out a six-point plan that calls for increased job creation, investments in competi-tiveness, improved education, dislocation insurance, and other similar measures.[25] I agree with it, and I recommend his arguments to our politicians.

Meanwhile, in every conceivable forum—in Congress, at the WTO, at the UN, at the World Bank, or wherever else we can put up a soapbox—we have to apply appropriate pressure on our trad-ing partners to do the right thing by their own workers, communi-ties, and environments. If we're going to play by the CSR rules, then so must they. If they don't, they should face the music—up to and including restricted access to our markets. Nothing is more in-furiating than to read about (for example) a Chinese pharmaceuti-cal manufacturer that exports cheap antitumor medicines to the United States but poisons the air and water in its hometown, thereby causing tumors and deformities in the local children.[26] The race to the bottom hurts not only American workers but also inno-cent kids in China.

Should we be willing to pull up the drawbridge, in cases like this, and risk being called protectionist? Let's just say drawbridges were invented to repel attacks. If we're attacked, we have to re-spond.

Closer to home, we absolutely have to rewrite our corporate tax laws to provide new incentives for American businesses to keep high-quality jobs in the United States. Today, corporations are taking advantage of tax loopholes to ship operations overseas and to shield profits earned abroad. And guess where those profits earned abroad ultimately get invested? Not in your neighborhood or mine!

Howls will go up in boardrooms around the country if these kinds of reforms begin to get serious consideration. Well, tough luck: *we have to eliminate the deferral of taxation on foreign-earned profits.* Period. It's the right thing to do, and it's the smart thing to do.

A Happy Ending

To a certain extent, responding to the challenges of outsourcing and offshoring is less a matter of thinking up new solutions and more a matter of making this issue a national priority. On a micro level, and in a hundred or a thousand different corporate settings, it's going to take a CEO with smarts, guts, and creativity to tackle these problems.

Like who? Well, like David Neeleman, founder and CEO of discount carrier JetBlue, who gives us a happy ending for what might otherwise feel like a pretty gloomy chapter. There *are* solutions to our problems, if we put our hearts and minds into finding them.

So who is David Neeleman? According to a very interesting article in *Forbes,* Neeleman used to work at Morris Air, a regional carrier that he also founded. In that earlier context, he started an experiment with at-home phone agents who made reservations and otherwise dealt with customers' requests, concerns, and complaints. His theory was simple enough: some people want to work at home. If Morris Air could give them the opportunity to do so, maybe they'd be more cheerful phone voices and more motivated problem-solvers. Good thinking, as it turned out; it worked.

When he founded JetBlue in 1998, Neeleman brought the idea along with him. Today, JetBlue employs seven hundred home-

based reservations agents. According to *Forbes,* the idea worked
again in this new context—and then some:

> Only one out of every 300,000 JetBlue passengers files a com-
> plaint for overbooking, baggage mishandling, or other customer
> service problems, compared with three for big carriers like Conti-
> nental and US Airways, according to federal data. Employees
> seem content. Agent turnover was only 4% last year, and the job
> is so popular that JetBlue rarely has to advertise to fill open posi-
> tions.[27]

What about the economics? And in the bigger scheme of things, do
we really care about seven hundred jobs at JetBlue?

The economics look pretty good. A traditional call center in the
United States costs something like $31 per hour, fully allocated,
whereas home-based agents cost about two-thirds as much.
JetBlue's home-based agents start at $8.25 per hour and earn all-
important benefits. (A job without benefits is like a car without
seats. More on benefits in our next chapter.) Yes, JetBlue could
probably cut those costs in half again by putting its call center in
some remote site on the far side of the world, as long as the people
there spoke reasonable English. But the airline business is nothing
if it's not a *service* business, and David Neeleman thinks that happy
Americans are in a better position to make other Americans happy.
The premium for hiring U.S. workers, he believes, is well worth it.

And do we give a damn about jobs in call centers? Well, the 4
million Americans who hold those jobs today certainly give a
damn. And we should be aware that whereas only 3,000 Indians
worked in call centers five years ago, that number has soared to
115,000 today and it's climbing rapidly.

And you know what? It should keep climbing. Those people
need and deserve jobs too, and they've been waiting a long time.
But all in all, at least 400,000 service jobs have moved offshore in
this same five-year period, with another 850,000 estimated to leave
our shores in 2005. We can't afford to shut down our domestic
economy in the interests of global equity. (All those Indians and
Chinese have a vested interest in a healthy U.S. economy, by the

way.) And we certainly can't afford to shut down our domestic economy to serve the exclusive interests of shareholders or—God forbid!—greedy management teams. God knows CEOs aren't *that* important.

We Americans are great workers. We work on average something like 350 hours a year—nine or ten weeks—more than Europeans, who are no slackers themselves.[28] We have big dreams, and we are willing to kill ourselves to realize those dreams. But it's not fair to ask us to run uphill. Make the playing field level, and those jobs will come home and stay home.

8

WAL-MART NATION?

When Ross Perot ran for president back in 1992, he coined a memorable political phrase. The passage of NAFTA, he said, would create a "giant sucking sound"—the sound of jobs being sucked out of the United States into Mexico.

As we saw in the last chapter, NAFTA proved only a short-lived boon for Mexico. By the year 2001, Mexican manufacturing wages had crept up to about $1.50 per hour. In isolation, this rate was certainly low enough to compete head-to-head with Americans, who enjoyed a minimum wage of better than three times that. But we no longer live in isolation. In China, at the turn of this century, manufacturing wages rarely exceeded 20 to 25 cents per hour.[1] The giant sucking sound now emanates from the Far East (and elsewhere), and those Mexicans, Hondurans, and others who benefited briefly from NAFTA can hear it clearly.

If you listen carefully, you can hear a second giant sucking sound. What is it? It's the sound of Wal-Mart—the world's largest company—sucking the vitality out of American families and communities, and out of our larger economy.

This loss happens in three different but related ways. First, there's the clobbering of Main Street: Wal-Mart moves in on the edge of town, and the downtown merchants—unable to match Wal-Mart's astounding purchasing power, and therefore unable to compete on price—soon go under. Second, there's the miserable benefits-and-wages package offered by Sam Walton's creation. Yes, you can find great bargains at Wal-Mart, but if you're a Wal-Mart employee, you may not be able to afford them. And third, there's Wal-Mart's purchasing strategy, which seems to involve buying American-made products only as a last resort.

Think about it. Wal-Mart, the spawn of Bentonville, Arkansas, commands an ever-larger share of retailing in the United States. It sucks up our hard-earned dollars—there's that vacuum-cleaner metaphor again—and sends them off to China to buy cheap stuff. Meanwhile, it drives down the standard of living of its own employees and of people working for companies that must compete with it. By shifting most of its purchasing offshore, it puts Americans out of work. And last but not least, Wal-Mart rules its suppliers with an iron fist.

You could make the case that we are well on our way toward turning into Wal-Mart Nation. But maybe we don't have to end up there. It's at least possible, if not likely, that Americans will wake up to the reality of Wal-Mart and embrace alternatives. A bit later in this chapter, I'll put one such alternative—Costco—on the table for consideration. No, Costco's not perfect. (No company is perfect.) But at least, in the spirit of corporate social responsibility, Costco acknowledges that it has responsibilities larger than simply enriching its owners.

A HISTORY LESSON

What is this powerful beast that we're wrestling with?[2] Sam Walton, born in Kingfisher, Oklahoma, in 1918, spent almost his entire life in retailing. Giving up on his youthful dreams of going to college, he became a management trainee with the J. C. Penney department-store chain in the late 1930s. After World War II, he opened a store—in Bentonville, Arkansas; population 20,000—that he franchised from the Ben Franklin chain. He gradually ex-

panded from this first toehold into a fifteen-store Ben Franklin operation, which established him as the biggest independent variety-
store operator in the United States.

But this was small potatoes, and Walton had far bigger dreams.
While operating his Ben Franklin stores, he had developed an early
version of the "everyday low prices" (EDLP) formula that would
later drive the Wal-Mart phenomenon. This innovation was
prompted, in large part, by the fact that the Ben Franklin headquarters added 25 percent to his wholesale prices. In order to overcome
this inherent price disadvantage and win more customers, Walton
had to generate enough economies to keep his prices reasonably
competitive. One way he did so was to order more merchandise
direct from the manufacturers, thereby eliminating middlemen.

In the early 1960s, Walton began hearing about a new phenomenon then centered in the northeastern United States: discount
retailing. This was basically the approach that today is called big-
box retailing: huge, no-frills stores stuffed full of merchandise at
low prices, offering little service beyond that provided at the check-
out counters.[3] After investigating this new approach—and after
seeing his own Ben Franklin store in Fayetteville, Arkansas, come
under pressure from a newly arrived discounter—Walton decided
to plunge into discount retailing himself. With his younger brother
Bud, he opened the first Wal-Mart Discount City Store in Rogers,
Arkansas, in 1962.

Rogers, Arkansas, you ask? Sam Walton singled out a second
relatively small city, in the northwest corner of a state that was
more or less overlooked until the rise of Bill Clinton, several decades later?

Well, yes, exactly, and this is a key thread in the Wal-Mart
story. The discounters that Walton studied had concentrated themselves in and around the big cities of the Northeast, and a high population density and short travel distances seemed to be essential
ingredients of their success. But Walton, a small-town boy himself,
was convinced that there was good money to be made by catering
to people in rural and semirural America. True, they didn't necessarily have the disposable income of those Yankees up north, but
hey, eventually they had to go shopping *somewhere,* and they had

to spend whatever money they had on the things they absolutely had to have. And country people were accustomed to driving long distances for a good price. If traditional retailers like Sears continued to be reluctant to build in the boonies, well, that might turn out to be a great niche.

It did.

And by the way, people in rural areas have relatively low salary expectations. Given the lack of many other competing payrolls in the hinterlands, Wal-Mart employees could be expected to be reasonably docile.

They were. In fact, the tilt away from wealthy, coastal America in favor of rural, lower-income America proved a critical factor in Wal-Mart's phenomenal growth. And the tilt continues today. "Of the over 230 SuperCenters opened in 2004," according to a Morgan Stanley research report, "only three were opened in California and just one in the Northeast Corridor."[4]

But I get ahead of myself. Wal-Mart was far from a meteoric success. Eight years after the company's founding, the chain consisted of only eighteen stores, all concentrated in the rural and semirural Southeast. But gradually, Sam Walton's retail savvy, his willingness to appropriate good ideas from competitors, his increasing purchasing power, his extraordinary personal energy level, his legendary tightfistedness, and his fanatical attention to detail combined to create a retailing phenomenon. Wal-Mart made major investments in technology, which accomplished several good ends at once. First, "shrinkage" (mostly pilferage either by shoppers or store employees) was minimized, because store managers could be held accountable for their inventories. Second, those inventories were replenished on a "just-in-time" basis, through computer links to manufacturers. Wal-Mart was able to avoid tying up dollars in unnecessary inventory, and at the same time it eliminated even more distributors and middlemen.

Wal-Mart's rivals, failing to see the writing on the wall, failed to make similar investments. Competitors like Kmart stumbled and fell. (In Kmart's case, the fall took the form of the largest retail bankruptcy in history, in early 2002.) And when they did fall, Wal-Mart was there to pick up the pieces.

Sam Walton, according to *Forbes,* became the richest man in the United States sometime in the mid-1980s. He and his family members retained nearly 40 percent of the company's stock, estimated to be worth something like $90 billion. And although Walton himself achieved cult-figure status within the company, his death in 1992 had no perceptible impact on Wal-Mart's fortunes. The pace of the juggernaut actually accelerated. Between 1988 and 2000, Wal-Mart's yearly revenues grew from $20 billion to $200 billion.

A short three years later, in part because of new revenues derived in Canada, Mexico, and Europe, sales had reached $245 billion. By this measure, Wal-Mart was the world's biggest company—twice as big as General Electric, and almost eight times as big as Microsoft. (Seen through a different lens, Wal-Mart ran a bigger "economy" than Ireland and Israel combined.) The company employed 1.4 million people worldwide, making it the world's largest private employer and, important to our review, the largest employer in twenty-five of the fifty United States. Twenty million shoppers a day visited its 4,688 stores, on average. Eighty percent of American households visited Wal-Mart at least once a year. In the 2003 Christmas season, Wal-Mart racked up its first billion-dollar sales days.

Keep in mind that there are legitimate reasons for all this success. By far, the most important of these is low prices, across a staggering assortment of goods. This is a blessing to consumers—although, as we will see, not an unmixed blessing.

Let's assume that Wal-Mart saves consumers 10 percent when it enters a new retail category—a reasonable assumption.[5] In other words, if Wal-Mart starts selling leaf blowers, you can now get a leaf blower at 90 percent of what you would have paid before Wal-Mart got into the leaf-blower business. Of its $245 billion of sales last year, if Wal-Mart did $200 billion in the United States—the actual breakouts by country are pretty closely guarded by the company, but this is probably a conservative figure—then Wal-Mart saved U.S. consumers something like $20 billion last year alone.

And that's far from the whole story. Since Wal-Mart has such enormous clout in the marketplace, the company keeps competitors' prices down as well, thereby saving consumers far more money. In fact, according to the *Financial Times,* the total savings to U.S. consumers generated directly and indirectly by Wal-Mart may exceed $100 billion annually.[6]

Well, who doesn't want to save their piece of that $100 billion? Who isn't willing to squint a little bit at the dark side of Wal-Mart—which, by now, most of us have heard something about—in order to cut 10 percent off the grocery bill?

"We have split brains," former Secretary of Labor Robert Reich told the *Los Angeles Times,* referring to our increasingly ambivalent attitude toward Wal-Mart. "Most of the time, the half of our brain that wants the best deal prevails."[7]

Wal-Mart has actually evolved into the evil it is today; it has gone from less bad to worse. For example, it wasn't always so ruthless in its pursuit of the cheapest possible goods, from anywhere in the world, no matter what the cost to American workers. In fact, in the mid-1980s, Sam Walton inaugurated a "Bring It Home to the USA" program, whereby his buyers would pay up to a 5 percent premium for U.S.-made goods. (In his memoirs, he boasted that he had created or saved some 100,000 American jobs through this program alone.)[8] But with the passage of NAFTA and other trade pacts, with the rise of internet-based commerce, and in the wake of Sam Walton's death, Wal-Mart quietly shelved its "Bring It Home" campaign.

Today, as we will see, Wal-Mart is just as ruthless as the next guy.

No, actually—more so.

CLOBBERING MAIN STREET
This coin that we're looking at definitely has two sides.

One side is Sam Walton: lovable old codger driving a beat-up pickup truck, sporting a blue and white Wal-Mart baseball cap, and never straying too far from his small-town roots, including the occasional quail hunt with his colorful cronies.

The other side is Wal-Mart employees chanting things like

Stack it deep
Sell it cheap
Stack it high
Watch it fly
Hear those downtown merchants cry![9]

Sometime in the early 1990s, people began to realize that falling in love with Wal-Mart entailed some negative consequences. It became increasingly clear that the arrival of a huge store on the outskirts of town with tons of free parking and "everyday low prices" posed a serious threat to the retailing status quo. Among the people most likely to be hurt by Wal-Mart were the long-established merchants in the kinds of small, isolated cities that the company preferred to target.

One of the first people to study this phenomenon was a professor of economics at Iowa State University named Ken Stone. In the mid-1980s, Stone began hearing anecdotally that downtown districts in his home state were atrophying in the wake of Wal-Mart's arrival. He launched a systematic study to find out what was really going on. The results were staggering—but again, not surprising. Iowa towns within a twenty-mile radius of a Wal-Mart experienced a 25.4 percent decline in total retail sales within five years of Wal-Mart's arrival. (Even outside that twenty-mile radius, retail sales fell by almost 18 percent within five years. As Sam Walton had guessed, country distances are shorter than city distances.) Certain store categories were even harder hit. Local hardware stores, for example, saw their sales decline by more than 30 percent.[10]

Others have reached more or less the same conclusion. "Within two years of a grand opening," wrote one longtime Wal-Mart critic, "Wal-Mart stores in an average-size Iowa town generated $10 million in annual sales—by 'stealing' $8.3 million from other businesses."[11]

Iowa's experience was, and is, representative—except that the clobbering of Main Street there may have happened a little more slowly than elsewhere. By contrast, Wal-Mart opened up in Rockland, Maine, in November 1992. During the month of December, Rockland enjoyed a 55 percent increase in total retail sales—most of which, of course, got rung up in Wal-Mart—while the four towns surrounding Rockland reported sales decreases ranging from 6 percent to 17 percent.[12]

Critics of what is sometimes called Sprawl-Mart also point out that the company's store-siting strategy leads inevitably to more sprawl and to the destruction of farmlands, open space, and natural habitats. This was the central argument used to block a proposed 250,000-square-foot Wal-Mart on the outskirts of Greenfield, Massachusetts, in 1993. That development was put to the voters of Greenfield, who—despite the $30,000 that Wal-Mart spent to influence the outcome of the election—turned it down.

The success of that Greenfield anti-Wal-Mart campaign inspired similar efforts in towns like East Aurora, New York; Palatine, Illinois; Mountville, Pennsylvania; Williston, Vermont; and Branford, Connecticut.[13] Even the National Trust for Historic Preservation has gotten into the act, arguing that big-box developments like Wal-Marts threaten the historic character of places like Vermont.

Question: How much land on the outskirts of scenic St. Albans, Vermont, does it take to put up a Wal-Mart (including its ample parking lots)?

Answer: Forty-four acres, give or take.

Question: How big is downtown St. Albans?

Answer: Forty-four acres, give or take.[14]

And what happens when Wal-Mart grows tired of a particular site? Again, it's one of those questions you might not want to ask.

Like a snake crawling out of its skin, Wal-Mart leaves these stores as a monument to redundant development. As of February 2004, Wal-Mart Realty is looking to lease or sell a total of 371 buildings, comprising 28,448,240 square feet of buildings, or 653 acres of empty buildings. Each store comes with at least as much parking lot space, so a minimum of 1,306 acres of land covered with impervious surface. Our scan shows that Wal-Mart now has empty stores in 37 states. Roughly half (49.9%) of these buildings, 185 stores, have been on the market for at least 2 years, and 21% (78 stores) have been sitting empty for 5 years or longer.

Just about one-third of these buildings, 117 stores (31.5%) are over 100,000 s.f. in size.[15]

Obviously, you need to decide for yourself whether you want to worry about suburban sprawl on the periphery of little cities and towns that you may never have occasion to visit. In a recent *Newsweek* column, pundit (and cynic) George F. Will mocked what he called the "liberal intelligentsia" for dumping on Wal-Mart and specifically for complaining about Wal-Mart's ravaging the suburban landscape.[16] He went on to point out that Wal-Mart was spending a billion dollars a month on U.S. real estate. That's a big number. What's your guess? How many of those dollars are going into brownfields and blighted urban neighborhoods?

Even if you don't worry much about blighted neighborhoods or brownfields, you may want to worry about how the world's biggest company is throwing its money and its political muscle around. In April 2004, voters in Inglewood, California, turned back an effort by Wal-Mart to get the local zoning code rewritten to its specifications. Two years earlier, the Inglewood City Council passed an ordinance limiting the percentage of nontaxable goods that a big-box store could carry. (The theory, apparently, was that the sale of nontaxable goods doesn't generate much in the way of tax revenues.) Wal-Mart not only got that ordinance rescinded but arranged to put a new seventy-one-page zoning plan—a plan of its own devising—in front of the voters. Then it spent more than $1 million to sway the vote.

It didn't work: Wal-Mart lost by a thumping three-to-two margin. (Getting a sixty/forty split on anything is tough; it's especially tough on complex issues like zoning ordinances.) "We are disappointed," admitted a Wal-Mart spokesman in the wake of the vote, "that a small group of Inglewood leaders together with representatives of outside special interests were able to convince a majority of Inglewood voters that they don't deserve the job opportunities and shopping choices that others in the LA area enjoy."[17]

Yes, but that's how democracy works. Local leaders take a stand, the voters vote, and—hopefully—the bad guys lose. It must have been one of those cases where people felt that some things are more important than "shopping choices." And maybe they had an inkling that those "job opportunities" aren't all they're cracked up to be either.

EXPLOITING WORKERS

Here's a topic that you could write a book about. (Many people have.) All this book can do is give the broad outlines of the case against the Giant of Bentonville.

Where to start? How about with the moral equivalent of indentured servitude? On October 23, 2003, FBI agents swooped down on sixty Wal-Marts in twenty-one U.S. states and arrested some 250 night-shift custodians whom the federal government accused of being illegal immigrants. Two weeks later, federal prosecutors notified Wal-Mart that it was under investigation, suspected of knowingly violating immigration laws. It wasn't the first such bust: in 1998 and again in 2001, the feds had rounded up a total of 102 custodians in U.S. Wal-Marts. This 2003 raid was notable for two reasons: it was more than twice as big as the first two combined, and it constituted a third strike against Wal-Mart, ultimately resulting in an $11 million settlement payment from Wal-Mart.[18]

The truly shocking story that emerged from this most recent bust, however, was the life that these janitors lived while under the Wal-Mart umbrella. Many had been recruited from Eastern European nations by means of a Web site that promised well-paying cleaning jobs in the United States. The Web site outreach program was operated by a cleaning contractor to which Wal-Mart subcontracted many of its cleaning services. Most of the recruits apparently thought they weren't doing anything wrong; they appeared to be pawns in a bigger corporate game.

One such recruit was a Czech citizen identified by the *New York Times* simply as Pavel. Pavel, jumping at the opportunity to earn four times what he was making as a restaurant manager in his home country, entered the United States on a tourist visa in February 2002. Following instructions, he hopped a bus to Lynchburg, Virginia, where the cleaning subcontractor delivered him to a local Wal-Mart. Assigned to the midnight shift, he started cleaning the

Wal-Mart for $380 a week, cash—or approximately $6.80 an hour, based on his fifty-six-hour weeks.

Eventually, after completing first one full week of work and then another, Pavel started wondering when he might get a day off. The answer? *Never.* He worked the graveyard shift *every night for the next eight months*—that is, right up to the night that the FBI shut down the cleaning operation.

The economics are compelling. If you run a cleaning service that doesn't pay taxes, Social Security, or workmen's compensation, you're in a pretty good position to win business from Wal-Mart. In fact, that may be the *only* way you're going to win the business, if others are playing by these cutthroat rules. No, Wal-Mart didn't force Pavel to work every single night for eight months for $6.80 an hour. Wal-Mart's contractor did that. But if you were Wal-Mart's CEO, would you want to have to hide behind that fig leaf?

OK, let's say that you are Wal-Mart's CEO and that you think that "once removed" is just fine. *(It wasn't me: it was my contractor.)* Then how about the jury in Oregon that concluded in 2002 that Wal-Mart managers had forced at least 290 workers to put in unpaid overtime? Using in-house satellite broadcasts, Bentonville would embarrass stores that were logging "too many" overtime hours. Managers at the offending stores would either tamper with employee time cards to cut back their hours or intimidate workers into working "off the clock." The Oregon case wasn't the first time this gambit reportedly had been employed either; Wal-Mart had previously settled out of court in similar cases in Colorado and New Mexico.[19]

It wasn't the last time either. By 2004, there were forty active lawsuits in twenty-five states accusing Wal-Mart of not paying employees the wages they had earned.[20]

But wait a minute: are we talking big wages here? Are we talking about cutting unproductive and overpaid workers down to size— knocking them back to a reasonable and competitive level of pay? Well, no. In fact, Wal-Mart pays very badly. According to a Harvard Business School case study, the average wage for a full-time Wal-Mart employee in 2002 was something less than $14,000. In that same year, according to the federal government, a family of three making less than $14,630 fell below the poverty line. Meanwhile, in 2002, Wal-Mart CEO Lee Scott earned a tidy $29 million, putting him in second place in that year's Fortune 50 list.[21]

And as for the "unproductive" part—not true either. Wal-Mart's overall sales per employee in 2003 averaged $175,000, while Kmart's employees sold an average of $145,000 and Target's sold $144,000.[22] Sure, Wal-Mart can point to its investments in information technology, training, and so on, and claim that it was those investments that led to such relatively productive workers. But unfortunately, there's no end to that logic. Why pay the workers minimum wage? Why pay the workers *anything*?

So much for involuntary servitude and pathetic wages; how about health insurance? Also not a pretty picture.

For better or worse, this country has a policy of making employers the first-line providers of health insurance. Nationwide, employers more or less step up to this responsibility, providing health-care benefits to 61 percent of their workers. Wal-Mart's comparable statistic? A paltry 38 percent. Remember, this is the company that *nets* $7 billion a year and counting.[23] As of 2002, you didn't even qualify for health coverage from Wal-Mart until you had worked at the company full-time for six months. (Where's a family supposed to go for coverage in the meantime?) Just to make it a little tougher, if you work fewer than thirty-four hours and fifty-two weeks a year, Wal-Mart classifies you as a part-timer, and you have to work two years before you're eligible for health coverage. And even after you qualify, you don't get very much:

> In 2002, Wal-Mart's spending on health benefits for the 500,000 employees covered in the United States averaged an estimated $3,500 per employee, versus $4,800 for the wholesale/retailing sector and $5,600 for U.S. employers in general.[24]

The problem here is that people making $7 an hour often decline to take even the health benefits they're offered, because they can't afford them. The result, of course, is that they stay uninsured, and the cost of their health care ultimately falls on the rest of us. Here's one explanation of exactly how that happens, courtesy of Ralph Nader's legions:

> In Georgia, one of 25 states where Wal-Mart happens to be the largest employer, over 10,261 children of Wal-Mart employees were recently found to be enrolled in the state's Peachcare program, which provides low-cost health insurance coverage to Georgia minors in families meeting federal poverty criteria. Six percent of Peachcare's September 2002 rolls (totaling 166,000 cases) were children from Wal-Mart families, blowing away the enrollment of the next highest private employer, Publix (734 families).[25]

A researcher at Rutgers University is undertaking a study to figure out exactly what it costs taxpayers in New Jersey (and by extension, elsewhere) to pick up the cost of uninsured retail workers' health care.[26] My confident prediction: it's not going to be a small figure. A group of University of California/Berkeley researchers published a study in August 2004 that concluded that in 2003, Wal-Mart's low wages and benefits cost California taxpayers $86 million in the form of food stamps, Medicare, and subsidized housing.[27] "In effect," the researchers concluded, "Wal-Mart is shifting part of its labor costs onto the public."[28]

And what do workers do when they decide that their company simply won't listen to them? Well, sometimes they organize. But if you try to organize at Wal-Mart, you put your own job, and maybe the jobs of your coworkers, at risk. That's what the meat cutters at Wal-Mart's Jacksonville, Texas, superstore discovered in 2000. Eleven days after they joined the United Food and Commercial Workers union, Wal-Mart announced that it was shutting down *all* of its meat-cutting operations at that store and switching to buying precut meat.[29]

As of 2004, only one of Wal-Mart's more than 4,000 North American stores—in Quebec, Canada—was unionized.[30] (As I was finishing this chapter, Wal-Mart announced that it was closing the store, allegedly for a lack of profitability.)[31] Wal-Mart uses no union labor to build its facilities, or—as we've seen—to clean them once they're built. None of Wal-Mart's 25,000 drivers is unionized, nor are the workers in its warehouses and distribution centers.[32]

Sam Walton—remember that lovable old codger with the baseball cap and the pickup truck?—once argued that his company ought to be exempted from the nation's minimum-wage laws.[33]

Where does this logic stop? Apparently, nowhere.

AMERICANS NEED NOT APPLY

If you're thinking about becoming a supplier of manufactured goods to the world's biggest company, you might want to think again. History suggests that you'll eventually have to ship your manufacturing jobs overseas, thereby hurting your American workers, or go out of business. And history further suggests that if you venture overseas, you'll be paying your new laborers next to nothing.

There are a million stories in this vein. One appeared in the on-line version of the magazine *Fast Company*, in an article by Charles Fishman.[34] Apparently, erstwhile clothing manufacturer Levi-Strauss—supplier of denims to the California Gold Rush, way back when—decided to climb into bed with Wal-Mart, essentially recasting its business practices to conform with Wal-Mart's "cheap at any price" approach. This decision entailed closing the company's last two U.S. factories and laying off more than 2,500 apparel workers. Today, Levi-Strauss is little more than an importer of cheap clothing manufactured in the Far East.

The *Los Angeles Times* told the story of a Chicago fan manufacturer that struggled to meet Wal-Mart's increasingly tough pricing demands. First, he automated production in the West Side factory that his grandfather had built, cutting his workforce from twenty-two to seven. Then, in 2000, he relocated much of his remaining manufacturing capacity to Shenzhen, China. Why? His Chicago-based workers earned $13 an hour; his Chinese workers made 25 cents an hour.[35]

In recent years, Wal-Mart has purchased something like $10 billion worth of Chinese-made goods, most of which were destined for resale in the United States. Maybe you won't be surprised to learn that Wal-Mart is actually driving down wages and benefits *even in China,* using the same tactics that it previously used in the United States: pitting one vendor against another and demanding either a quality improvement or a price reduction every year. And while Wal-Mart maintains that all of its global suppliers adhere to a corporate "code of conduct," which supposedly safeguards against exploitive practices, it also refuses to identify its global suppliers—which, of course, prevents independent confirmation of adherence to any code of conduct.[36]

Nevertheless, investigators have tracked down a number of Wal-Mart suppliers that don't conform to any particular code of conduct. Here's what the National Labor Committee—a labor-rights advocacy group—reported about a factory in China's Guangdong Province that manufactures action figures and other toys sold by Wal-Mart:

13- to 16-hour days molding, assembling, and spray-painting toys from 8 a.m. to 9 p.m. or even midnight, seven days a week, with 20-hour shifts in peak season.

Even though China's minimum wage is 31 cents an hour—which doesn't begin to cover a person's basic subsistence-level needs—these production workers are paid 13 cents an hour.

Workers typically live in squatter shacks, seven feet by seven feet, or jammed in company dorms, with more than a dozen sharing a cubicle costing $1.95 a week for rent. They pay about $5.50 a week for lousy food. They also must pay for their own medical treatment and are fired if they are too ill to work.

The work is literally sickening, since there's no health and safety enforcement. Workers have constant headaches and nausea from paint-dust hanging in the air; the indoor temperature tops 100 degrees; protective clothing is a joke; repetitive stress disorders are rampant; and there's no training on the health hazards of handling the plastics, glue, paint thinners, and other solvents in which these workers are immersed every day. . . .

These factories employ mostly young women and teenage girls.[37]

"Sickening" is the right word. When we talk about creating a level playing field for competition in the world marketplace, this is what we're talking about. Can American workers compete with Chinese teenagers working under these conditions?

Should they?

For that matter, should American consumers exploit Chinese kids?

Careful: if you say no, you may have to change your shopping patterns.

THE ISSAQUAH ALTERNATIVE

Is there another way to go? Maybe. The first step toward taming Wal-Mart will come in a language that the Bentonville Behemoth understands: the language of a competitive threat.

From Wal-Mart's perspective, the scariest thing on the horizon is a scrappy "little" company called Costco Wholesale. (Only in comparison to Wal-Mart is a $42 billion company puny.) Costco is scary to Wal-Mart because the Issaquah, Washington–based retailer runs better warehouse clubs than Wal-Mart. I'm guessing that Costco is also scary to Wal-Mart because Costco has found a way to treat its workforce like human beings.

First, the competitive numbers: in 2003, Wal-Mart had 532 Sam's Club warehouse stores, which did about $33 billion in sales. Not bad—except that Costco had only 312 stores and did $34.5 billion in sales.[38] Hmmm, 40 percent fewer outlets and 5 percent more sales. *That's* interesting.

Here's some more interesting statistics:

- Costco's pay scale *begins* at $10 per hour. (Wal-Mart's hourly average is $9.96, although this figure doesn't include Sam's Club wages, which the company does not reveal.) After four years, a Costco cashier can be earning $44,000, counting bonuses.
- Costco covers 92 percent of its employees' health-care costs and makes benefits available to most of its employees.
- One in every six Costco workers belongs to a union.

• Turnover at Costco (17 percent) is far less than half that at Wal-Mart (44 percent).

• Costco's U.S. operating profit per hourly employee in 2003 was $13,647, versus $11,039 at Sam's Club. Labor costs as a percentage of sales are actually lower at Costco than at Wal-Mart, despite Costco's significantly higher wage structure.

• Between 2003 and 2004, Costco's same-store sales were up 10 percent; at Wal-Mart, they were up only 2.4 percent.

• Markups at Costco average 10 percent, versus approximately 20 percent at Wal-Mart.[39]

Costco's CEO Jim Sinegal tells interviewers that his employees made the company what it is today. It's only fair, he says, that they should share in the profits. "They're entitled to buy homes and live in reasonably nice neighborhoods and send their children to school," he commented early in 2004.[40] And as he explained to *BusinessWeek,* Sinegal also has his eye on larger societal trends that he finds worrisome:

> If current trends persist, a greater and greater share of wealth will keep going into the hands of the few, which will destroy initiative. We'll no longer have a motivated working class.[41]

"I'm a big admirer of Wal-Mart, but I admire Costco more," said Charles Munger, in an interview with *USA Today.* Munger is Warren Buffett's longtime business associate, and he also sits on Costco's board. "Virtually none of the sins of modern capitalism are at Costco."[42]

"Employees are willing to do whatever it takes to get the job done," says one seventeen-year Costco veteran.[43]

So there you have it: the Issaquah alternative. A humane and broad-gauge CEO; a proud board member with a good sense of the real-world alternatives; and a fully motivated employee. It all sounds good, and realistic.

Again, Costco isn't perfect. The company faces accusations of bias against women in its promotion policies, with some 650 women seeking redress. (Wal-Mart is facing a similar suit that may involve up to 1.6 million women.)[44] Meanwhile, Wall Street complains about the company's inexplicable determination to treat its people like people. "At Costco," grumbles Bill Dreher, an analyst with Deutsche Bank, "it's better to be an employee or a customer than a shareholder."[45]

Fair enough. But where would *you* rather work—Costco or Wal-Mart?

And I note with interest that between January 2004 and January 2005, Costco's share price went up a pretty respectable 30 percent. Not bad, all things considered.[46]

PUSHING FROM BEHIND

Let's not kid ourselves. Over here, on this side of the scale, put Costco and Target and Sears, Roebuck and Kmart. Over there, put Wal-Mart. Now watch the scale tip dramatically in Wal-Mart's direction: its sales are 50 percent greater than those of all these competitors combined.[47]

So we're dealing with an enormously powerful economic (and political) engine, and one that's not likely to change its direction anytime soon. Change will require creative leaders at other companies—like Costco's Jim Sinegal—to come up with economically viable alternatives to the Wal-Mart model. Meanwhile, it will require investors who are willing to demand a little less and shoppers who are willing to pay a little more. It's not going to be easy. Here's an ugly little set of facts from *Business Week:*

> Wal-Mart's other strategy [for fixing the problems described above] might simply be to weed out managers found to have acted improperly and, when necessary, introduce reforms. The drawback, of course, is that the cost of such measures could alarm Wall Street, which usually doesn't award points for being nice to employees. If the cost of such changes amounted to a measly $1 an hour for each of Wal-Mart's 1.2 million employees, the bill would total $2.1 billion a year. That could reduce Wal-Mart's profits by about 25%—or force it to raise prices and lessen its advantage in the marketplace.[48]

In other words, retailing is a tough game, in which an extra dollar an hour across the workforce whacks profits by 25 percent. So among other things, it's going to take enlightened leadership at Wal-Mart itself to stop the company's irresponsible practices and to pursue policies that—despite irritating Wall Street—acknowledge a broader range of responsibilities than simply enriching the company's owners.

One button I'd push, if (God forbid!) I were heading up Wal-Mart, is turnover. It's good that Wal-Mart managed to cut its turnover rate down from 70 percent annually in 1999 to 44 percent in 2003. The lingering recession probably had a lot to do with that reduction. But 44 percent of 1.4 million is still 600,000 new people that Wal-Mart has to hire and train every year, just to stay even.[49] That's a staggering number, especially since Wal-Mart estimates that it costs an average of $2,500 to find and train a new hire.[50] Memo to Wal-Mart: Treat people better so they won't leave, and you can keep your eye trained on building for the future rather than training against employee turnover.

Another button I'd push is the cost of bad PR. As of 2003, Wal-Mart was spending something like $700 million a year on ads—partly to attract shoppers, of course, but also to buff up its tarnished image.[51] The cost of that buffing will go up every year, perhaps geometrically, unless the company starts behaving itself. Wouldn't it be better to spend that money on employees and their communities and on making things better than to spend it on spinmeisters and local TV stations in a foredoomed effort to unconvince people of things they already know?

Ultimately, it will take a CEO with guts and vision, and he or she almost certainly will need a lot of pushing from behind. You and me—all of us—are going to have to insist that the world's biggest company do a whole lot better. And when Wal-Mart does better, that will allow other companies to do better too.

9

PUTTING THE HEALTH BACK IN HEALTH CARE

Scrutinizing Wal-Mart gave us the opportunity to dig down deep into its operating practices and to get a sense of the far-ranging impact of those practices on employees and families, communities, states, and even the national economy. Presumably, readers in Georgia and California—where investigators have dug down far deeper—took note of how expensive Wal-Mart's vaunted "everyday low prices" can really be at the state level.

But Wal-Mart isn't the only company that plays and shifts the costs of its own responsibilities onto others. In this chapter, we will look across a broader range of companies and at a particular range of responsibilities that companies ought to own up to but in many cases don't—the responsibilities for health care. Where possible, I will point to creative corporate practices that are putting the health back in health care—and even using health-care benefits packages creatively to advance both corporate and societal goals.

THE BENEFIT YOU CARE MOST ABOUT: HEALTH CARE

The most important employment-related benefit, of course, is health insurance.[1] Approximately 45 million Americans have no health insurance at all. In the first two years of the twenty-first century, the number of uninsured under the age of sixty-five grew by 3.7 million, or almost 10 percent.[2] These uninsured people are not necessarily poor, inner-city residents or recent immigrants or even unemployed workers. According to the *New York Times,*

> The majority of the uninsured are neither poor by official standards nor unemployed. They are accountants . . . employees of small businesses, civil servants, single working mothers, and those working part time or on contract.[3]

The *Wall Street Journal,* similarly, reported on an analysis of data derived from the U.S. Census Bureau. This analysis suggested that of the current 45 million uninsureds, 70 percent either work full-time or are the dependents of people working full-time, and 30 million or so—well more than half—are from households with annual incomes of more than $25,000.[4] Again, the uninsureds don't conform to any neat stereotype.

But they do add up. The state of Texas has the highest proportion of uninsured citizens in the country: one in four. The lingering nationwide recession contributed to a $10 billion budget shortfall in Texas in 2003. This gap led to cuts in state subsidies for health insurance, which led in turn to the loss of $500 million in federal support. (When a state fails to meet its obligations, the feds cut back on theirs.) The ultimate consequence? More than a half million Texas children who previously had received subsidized dental, vision, and mental-health care lost their coverage. If the crummy economic conditions that prevail at this writing persist through 2005, then, according to one analysis, something like 170,000 kids in Texas will lose *all* their health coverage.[5]

Perhaps not surprisingly, our medical establishment has started to play hardball with uninsured people who can't pay their bills. The *Wall Street Journal* recently chronicled the story of a number of U.S. hospitals that are resorting to the courts to jail, garnish the wages, and seize the tax refunds of people who fall behind on their medical bills. One uninsured musician in the Champaign-Urbana, Illinois, area, for example, seriously wounded himself in a failed suicide attempt. When he missed a hearing on his overdue hospital bill of $7,718, the hospital to which he owed the money—the not-for-profit Carle Foundation Hospital—asked the court to issue a warrant for the musician's arrest. He was, in fact, arrested and jailed briefly.[6]

There's another irony in this story. Keep in mind that HMOs, PPOs, and other insurance-company-supported plans have considerable purchasing power with hospitals and therefore are able to negotiate relatively good rates for their insured populations. So that bill of $7,718 was almost certainly far higher than it would have been for an insured person under identical circumstances. In a similar case, an uninsured woman making $19,000 a year underwent an emergency appendectomy at New York's Beth Israel Hospital in July 2002. This woman was charged full freight for her lifesaving procedure and subsequent brief hospital stay: $24,000.[7] And USA Today wrote up the story of an uninsured Florida man who spent seventeen days in a hospital and got socked with a bill for $116,000. That same hospital would have charged an insurance company just $25,000 for the same services.[8]

On a personal note, I recently had what seemed like a few minor diagnostic tests: walk in, lie down, get scanned, talk with the doc, and go home again. The bill? Almost $2,500. The cost to me? Less than $150. Good deal! And I'm willing to bet that for an uninsured person, that $2,500 bill would have been higher.

It has come to this: we're charging the most desperate people the highest fees—sometimes as much as 500 percent more than their insured counterparts. When the American Hospital Association claimed that federal government rules *required* them to charge full freight—and to play tough with slow payers—then–Health and Human Services secretary Tommy Thompson wrote a strongly worded letter saying that the rules required no such thing. And, he added pointedly, HHS was then (in calendar year 2003) providing $22 billion in annual subsidies to help care for the uninsured.[9] *Billion* with a *b*, paid for with your federal tax dollars, which of course are in addition to whatever we're paying for our own health insurance.

The truly scary thing is that when it comes to the dreadful state of health care in the United States today, these sobering statistics and anecdotes dramatically understate the problem. Yes, it's dis-graceful that in the world's richest country, hundreds of thousands of kids in Texas and elsewhere are being put at risk through no fault of their own. And it's terrible that a single procedure—admittedly a lifesaving one—can cost more than a year's salary, or that you may be hauled off to jail for failure to pay the resulting as-tronomical hospital bills. But it's also terrible that many of the fam-ilies and individuals who *are* covered are paying way too much and getting way too little.

And finally, putting my CEO hat on for a moment, it's terrible that it costs General Motors upward of $67 billion a year to pro-vide health benefits to its retirees—an annual liability that is more than double the company's entire market capitalization. And GM is not alone, of course. Three out of five U.S. employers admit to wanting to go shopping for a new and better plan.[10] The problem is, they won't find one, at least not under current circumstances.

How many consumers in America today are totally satisfied with their health-care situation? Not many. The reasons are obvi-ous. In the United States today, we have a patchwork health-care system that is primarily designed to respond to emergencies and acute illnesses. We have chosen to make employers the insurers of first resort. But they're not particularly good at it, and the need to be profitable (and to limit the damage imposed by health care) compels them to offer only a limited menu. Today, most large com-panies offer only a single plan, or several plans that are more or less indistinguishable; almost all small companies (more than nine out of ten, according to recent estimates) offer only one plan.

Sometimes politicians pretend that this whole clunky system grew out of some strong moral imperative and therefore needs to be defended at all costs. But that's simply not the case. Corporate involvement in the provision of health care was an almost inciden-tal by-product of World War II–era price controls. In other words, it was an accident of history, and employers would now dearly love to mitigate the adverse effects of this accident.[11]

What else is wrong? The system stresses fighting illness and puts very little emphasis on promoting wellness. Why? Because the system is not designed to promote wellness. It's too reactive and too fragmented.

As many people before me have pointed out, this approach is self-defeating. By delivering health care this way, we first fail to head off ailments that could have been avoided entirely. Then we fail to minimize the costs of treating people with those ailments. Meanwhile, we're incurring enormous costs in the form of absenteeism and reduced effectiveness on the job. Here's an interesting analysis, courtesy of Professor Regina E. Herzlinger, writing in the *Harvard Business Review*:

> Most health care expenditures are spent on treating chronic conditions and their complications. In 1996, according to *Health Affairs,* just five diseases—mood disorders, diabetes, heart disease, hypertension, and asthma—accounted for 49 percent of total expenditures and caused an additional $36 billion in work-related losses.[12]

That's right: five predictable and relatively manageable diseases chew up fully half of our health-care dollars and cost another $36 billion beyond that. Throw in cancer, arthritis, AIDS, and a few others, and you get to something like 80 percent of all health-care dollars! It's a shameful situation. These are diseases that need to be headed off, where possible. What did Ben Franklin say? An ounce of prevention is worth a pound of cure. But by the time we're done reacting to the treatable, we have very little money left for prevention.

Where prevention is not possible, diseases and conditions need to be managed. Unfortunately, management often requires a team of health-care providers who bring a variety of different specializations to the table. But in today's fragmented system, it falls to the patient to figure out what's needed and when. This burden can be scary, confusing, and frustrating. Things, and people, fall through the cracks. "According to one study," reports Herzlinger, "only 36 percent of fully insured elderly diabetics . . . receive a biannual glycosylated hemoglobin test, even though it's essential to their well-being."[13] In other words, if you don't get this test, you'll cost the system lots more money, your quality of life will deteriorate, and you may die prematurely. And remember, these are the *fully insured*, failing to figure out or get what they need, and suffering, and costing the system a ton of money. It's disgraceful.

What is to be done? Well, as President Clinton learned early in his tenure, what's *not* likely to be done is a radical overhaul of the health-care delivery system in the United States. There are simply too many powerful forces arrayed against such a change—even if in the long run it stood to benefit all parties. *Question:* Which organization came in number three in total lobbying dollars spent in Washington in the last six months of 2000, second only to the Business Roundtable and General Electric? *Answer:* The American Medical Association.[14] All told, the AMA spent $17 million on Capitol Hill that year, a decent slug of the $209 million spent by all health-care lobbyists working the halls of Congress. Members of Congress are outnumbered thirteen to one by health-care lobbyists.[15] No wonder radical reform appears to be a lost cause.

One interesting "lost cause" is a plan put forward recently by Ezekiel J. Emanuel, an oncologist and bioethicist affiliated with the National Institutes of Health, in collaboration with retired Stanford economist Victor R. Fuchs. (In other words, two smart guys, well wired, with no particular ax to grind.) Emanuel and Fuchs argue for getting employers out of the health-care loop entirely. Employer-sponsored health plans, they point out, necessarily mean that the burden of choosing plans falls on the employer, and health benefits aren't sufficiently portable.

How would their alternative system work? First, health-care vouchers would be issued to all Americans. Yes, overnight, *everyone in the United States would be insured.* Just like that. And no, this would not be the end of the private health-care system. People would simply use their vouchers to purchase policies tailored to their specific needs—more of this, less of that. If an individual required extra services beyond those encompassed by that policy, he or she would pay a premium (but not, God forbid, full freight!) for that service. Emanuel and Fuchs claim that all in, such a system would cost the government on the order of $840 billion, which is substantially less than the $1.4 trillion it is paying today.[16]

Once again, we should listen for the howls going up: *Another plan to nationalize health care! Another plan for the bloated federal bureaucracy to take away your right to choose, thereby eviscerating the best health-care system in the world!*

Well, that's not what Emanuel and Fuchs propose. And it's easy to make the case that we *don't* have the best health-care system in the world. But that's for another book. In the meantime, what's an intermediate proposal that might not generate instant and overwhelming opposition and might get us moving in the right direction?

Harvard's Professor Herzlinger has put forward an interesting meet-you-halfway sort of proposal, which requires both employer and employee involvement. First, her rationale: she argues that as long as the health-care industry remains shielded from direct consumer pressure, it will remain bloated, overpriced, and unresponsive. No matter what the industry, she contends, consumers force innovation, which very quickly leads to higher productivity, lower costs, improved quality, and increased choices. She points to the revolution that occurred when corporate America shifted from defined benefit retirement plans (pensions) to defined contribution plans (401(k)s, SEPs, IRAs, and so on). Choices proliferated, prices for executing stock trades and other services plummeted, and—although the jury is still out—consumers appear to have derived some significant benefits.

How does this principle translate into health care? Herzlinger presents a hypothetical scenario:

> An employer gives its employees the sum it would have spent on their health benefits or lets them contribute their own pretax funds, or both. Employees will be required to use some of that money to purchase, at a minimum, an insurance policy that protects them against financially catastrophic medical events. They will then have considerable flexibility in using the balance to purchase other insurance or care options. Employees who face large, uninsured, out-of-pocket expenses, for example, can trade off the money now spent on insurance coverage they don't want for the things they need.[17]

Herzlinger seems confident that people will have the wisdom and time needed to make good health-care choices. I don't share that confidence, especially because health care is one of those areas where a seemingly small mistake can turn out to be a catastrophic one. The analogy to IRAs and 401(k)s is also not comforting. One thing that has become increasingly clear in recent years is that defined contribution plans are generally less valuable to retirees than the defined benefit plans they have replaced. (Think about it: why else would corporations have embraced defined contributions so wholeheartedly?) We for sure don't want health care to go the same route.

Nevertheless, it's very appealing to contemplate people gaining more control over their health-care dollars, and—by extension— over the design of their particular health-care strategy. (Yes, it's time to start using the word *strategy* when thinking about health care.) Who do you think is more likely to understand your family's circumstances and make good choices based on that understanding—the overtaxed staffers in your company's HR department or you? Assuming that you get the information and other resources that you'll need, you should bet on yourself every time.

In fact, this is the thinking that lies behind some of the more interesting health-care reforms currently being floated by corporations. For lack of a better term, call it consumer-driven health care. The idea is to give consumers better information about individual providers—doctors and hospitals—and let *them* find the effective and efficient resources. This impulse explains the recent big push to release previously confidential government ratings on the safety and efficacy of individual hospitals: give consumers the information they need and deserve.

At the same time, some of these companies give consumers extra dollars to buy services not ordinarily covered by health plans, with an eye toward promoting wellness. Alternatively, they bring wellness programs in-house and offer employees incentives for participating in them and hitting established benchmarks.

And as the third leg of this stool, some employers offer physicians and other care providers a flat, per-head fee for providing certain kinds of preventive care. "In California," reports the *Financial Times,* "the Integrated HealthCare Association offers bonuses to doctors who screen their patients for cervical and breast cancer, coronary artery problems, and other conditions that are expensive to treat."[18] The IHA has also undertaken an ambitious initiative to evaluate 215 California-based medical groups, as part of the state's larger Pay for Performance (PFP) program. Between $50 million and $100 million in bonuses will be awarded to top-performing groups—and all of this information is being made available to the public.[19]

Again, it's easy to find fault with these kinds of efforts. Paying bonuses to doctors who keep their patients well tends to give those doctors a perverse incentive: *Weed out the really sick ones ahead of time and protect that bonus!* And once again, it's not good enough to simply send people out into the world with cash, credits, vouchers, and so on, if you don't also take responsibility for fully educating people about their choices.

CO-PAYS: DUMB WAYS, SMART WAYS

We've moved from the most audacious plan, to a less audacious plan, and have now arrived at tinkering at the margins—which, modest as it sounds, is still much better than doing nothing.

So let's assume again that history is our best guide and that there is no radical reform in our national approach to health care waiting around the next bend in the road. So what can we do in the meantime?

We can undertake piecemeal reforms that—although far from comprehensive—will improve the picture. As suggested above, the guiding philosophy of these reforms should be to help consumers understand where their medical dollars are going and to help them spend those dollars wisely. And as our case study, let's look at co-payments for prescription drugs.

In May 2004, the *Journal of the American Medical Association* published the results of a Rand Corporation study that examined the cost of increased co-payments for prescription drugs. It turns out that using co-payments as a blunt instrument to contain health-care costs leads to a whole universe of unintended and mostly adverse consequences.[20]

By now, everyone understands that something has to be done about the runaway costs of prescription drugs. For the past decade or two, we've been trapped in an upward cost spiral in this subset of health care, with new drugs coming on the market, with drug companies ratcheting up prices for their products with doctors prescribing brand-name (rather than generic) products and with consumers failing to pay much attention to the actual costs of those medications. (After all, someone else is footing the bill, right?) One embarrassing result is the busloads of retirees making trips to Canada to buy prescription drugs at a fraction of their cost in the United States. At the risk of stating the obvious, nobody—not the politicians, not the drug companies—wants to see those buses again and again on the evening news.

In the old days, health-plan subscribers were required to pay a single low co-payment, often in the range of five dollars, no matter what kind of prescription they needed to get filled. But over the last decade or so, in an effort to control their skyrocketing costs, most employers and insurers have developed a complicated classification system for drugs, with a sliding scale of associated co-payments. Today, drugs are defined as either generic, preferred branded, or nonpreferred branded, and the associated co-payments tend to be around $10, $20, and $40, respectively.

The Rand study examined data covering 530,000 people at thirty companies over a three-year period. For that group, in that time period, co-pays went up by 100 percent: from $6.31 to $12.62 for generic drugs, and from $12.85 to $25.70 for brand-name drugs. What was the result?

> When co-payments doubled, the use of prescription drugs fell between 17% and 23% among patients with diabetes, asthma, and gastric acid disease. Meanwhile, visits to emergency rooms rose 17% for people with those conditions, and hospital stays increased 10%.[21]

Remember those chronic diseases we talked about earlier? Well, it turns out that if we make certain kinds of prescription drugs significantly more expensive, then lots of people with those chronic diseases stop taking their medications, and close to one in five winds up getting hospitalized as a result and staying longer in the hospital. Have you looked at the cost of a night in a hospital bed recently? Remember the $24,000 appendectomy described earlier?

Let's assume that a night in the hospital, including tests and other charges, is a thousand bucks—certainly on the low side, but it's a nice round number to work with. So one night in a hospital wipes out the increased co-payments on 158 generic prescriptions ($1,000/$6.31), or on 78 branded prescriptions ($1,000/$12.85). Meanwhile, it's probably safe to assume that emergency-room visits and hospital overnights aren't the only increased health-care costs that tend to crop up when people stop taking their meds. What about increased absenteeism? What about more doctor visits? What about greater demands on psychiatric services and other kinds of counseling?

So just upping co-pays across the board appears to be dumb, as well as cold-blooded. But what are the alternatives?

The *Wall Street Journal* points to two. In 2000, office-machine maker Pitney Bowes Inc. began offering its employees certain critical medicines—such as those needed to treat diabetes and asthma—at 10 percent of their retail cost. Based on subsequent analyses, this single move led directly to a reduction in emergency-room visits and hospital stays (that is, lower overall costs).

Worthington Industries, a metals processor, rebates health-care premiums to employees who participate in the company's health-maintenance program. Employees with treatable conditions, such as high blood pressure, set goals for eliminating or minimizing the threats to their health. When they hit those goals, they win: better health. So does the insurance company and the employer: lower costs.

The lesson of these and similar stories is not that co-pays are bad or that they should not be used as tools to help achieve certain ends. Basic economics are at play here: when there's no connection between the cost of a good and its consumption, people tend to consume more (and more expensively) than they absolutely need to. When the cost of gasoline goes through the roof, you cut back on unnecessary trips and refrain from stomping down on the gas pedal. Tiered co-payment schedules are like those big numbers on the top of the gas pump. They're a small step—but a necessary one—toward reestablishing a link between the cost of a medicine and the consumer's pocketbook.

They're not a good thing when people are steered toward unsatisfactory medicines simply because of their lower cost. Psychopharmacology (the realm of medicines that affect thought and emotions) is a case in point. Ask any clinician who cares for people with emotional and affective disorders: in many circumstances, the generic drugs simply aren't good enough. Especially in this unhappy realm, unwelcome side effects or reduced efficacy can lead to disaster.

Still, co-payments can get us a little closer to linking up consumers and costs, if they are used selectively and creatively.

DOMESTIC PARTNER BENEFITS:
WHY IS THIS SO DAMN DIFFICULT?

Doing the right thing makes economic as well as moral sense when it comes to co-payments for prescription drugs. Now let's look at a corner of the benefits arena where it's harder to make the case that doing the right thing makes economic sense and yet we have to do the right thing anyway. And beyond the morality of the issue, of course, we can point to indirect benefits to the corporation, which almost certainly translate into dollars earned or saved, somewhere down the line.

Here, we're talking about benefits for the domestic partners of employees—which in the ear of the public often translates into "the gay partners of gay employees." (As we'll see, though, that situation is the exception rather than the rule.) Way back in 1982, the *Village Voice*—the ultrahip newspaper based in New York's Greenwich Village—offered what it called "domestic partner" benefits to the unmarried partners of its employees (whether of the same sex or the opposite sex). The always-progressive city of Berkeley, California, followed suit three years later.[22] Beginning in the early nineties, a number of enlightened companies decided to go the same route. Today, something like 7,400 employers offer domestic partner benefits. Most of these (around 6,800) are private-sector companies, including, it should be noted, only around 200 of the Fortune 500.[23]

Here's the current reality: about a third of current partner-benefit plans are available only to same-sex domestic partners. Most of the other two-thirds are open to domestic partners of any gender, and overall about two-thirds of the people taking advantage of domestic partner benefits are opposite-sex partners. Almost inevitably, though, the partner-benefit debate has focused on the homosexual minority rather than on the heterosexual majority. I'll focus on that minority as well, since that's where my own relevant managerial experiences were concentrated and where most of the current legal struggles are centered.

Let me make an extended personal digression to underscore some important points. Based on the anecdotal evidence I've seen, my former company—InterMedia—was one of the first organizations in the U.S. private sector to offer domestic partner benefits. Back when we first took this step, there was almost no body of case law establishing a legal connection between a gay employee and his or her partner. In other words, CEOs couldn't be compelled to do anything for unmarried partners. (In fact, they still can't, for the most part.) So if your lover got AIDS and you were the employee, well, no spillover to the company—other than your own grief, of course, and perhaps seeing yourself get destroyed financially.

That's how most CEOs looked at the issue back then. Unfortunately, that's how many of them still look at it today, maybe including the leaders of those other 300 companies in the Fortune 500.[24]

We saw it differently—although I'm the first to admit that I personally didn't get there right away. Before I went to TCI, I helped run Chronicle Publishing Company in San Francisco from 1985 until 1988. Then, in 1988, I founded my own cable television company, InterMedia, also headquartered in San Francisco. In both businesses, we had a wonderful employee community—more like a large extended family than a typical workforce—and I learned a lot. (One of my earliest friends at Chronicle, and later my mentor, was the courageous journalist Randy Shilts, who alerted our city and then the nation to a new disease called AIDS.) I also had the great pleasure of getting to know the partners of many of my gay and lesbian associates, as well as of my heterosexual associates. For me, it was enlightening to see how comfortable and tolerant people of every stripe were with one another. At the same time, I can honestly say that once you got welcomed into these employee communities, you never gave someone's sexual orientation a second thought. Nor, as far as I know, did they worry about yours.

These experiences taught me a valuable lesson regarding the rewards that come with embracing diversity. I became much more aware and accepting of lifestyles and cultural practices different from my own. I met exceptional people whom to this day I count among my dearest friends.

All of this experience got me to thinking more deeply. I started imagining what my life would be like if straight people (like me) faced the kinds of prejudice experienced by gays or lesbians. What if it would be career-threatening to have pictures of my wife, or my child, on my desk? What if the discovery of my heterosexuality might derail my prospects for promotion? Suppose I had to maintain a low profile in order to avoid being discovered for what I was. Would I be able to give the full measure of my talents to my employer? And if benefits were denied to my wife and family, would I be able or even inclined to do my best on behalf of the company?

What I was imagining was a workplace without justice. All in all, it was a stark and ugly vision. As a lone CEO, of course, I couldn't undo centuries of prejudice and discrimination. But I surely could put a stop to injustices that grew out of our own corporate practices. So, almost immediately upon my arrival at Chronicle and immediately upon founding InterMedia, I extended benefits to the domestic partners of our employees. This wasn't a very popular move with some of my more conservative colleagues at Chronicle. In fact, some of them disagreed vociferously—mostly on the grounds that this was an inappropriate use of corporate resources. I heard them out and then told them I disagreed.

When I arrived at the much, much larger TCI in February 1997, I brought my convictions along with me. I immediately instituted the same zero-tolerance policy regarding any form of discrimination against any of our employees that I had established at

InterMedia. I communicated, forcefully and whenever possible in person, the message that if any employee was discovered practicing intolerance, discrimination, or intimidation against another, his or her career at TCI was finished. Simply put, discrimination was a career ender. And once again, I introduced partner benefits as quickly as possible.

People are people are people. Treat them fairly, and your own life is enriched. Treat your employees fairly and equally, and your company is enriched and more successful.

It's hard to fathom why so many companies find these basic concepts so difficult to grasp. Part of it must be a simple miscalculation of the economics. Most likely, some green-eyeshade types sitting in basements somewhere have decided that gay people are at greater risk of contracting AIDS and therefore represent a greater health-care liability to the company than straight people. But this not only misreads the current state of the AIDS epidemic, it also fails to look at the other side of the gay/straight calculation. Think only people who might get AIDS are expensive? Try people who might get pregnant. They can be *really* expensive.[25]

In fact, providing partner benefits is much less expensive than many people expect. For one thing, not all that many people enroll, and when they do, it doesn't really cost all that much. According to a 2000 study by benefits experts Hewitt Associates, something like 1.2 percent of all eligible employees wind up enrolling their partners in their health plan, and the overall cost increase for 85 percent of all participating companies is less than 1 percent.[26] At Boston's Beth Israel Deaconess Medical Center, only 40 out of 5,000 employees take advantage of the hospital's domestic partner coverage.[27] At Emory University, it is 50 out of 14,000 employees—not exactly a flood tide.[28]

But you can't overlook the fact that many companies are simply tone-deaf—or perhaps ethics-starved. How about the fact that Home Depot—one of America's truly hot companies and stocks in recent years—until very recently declined to offer partner insurance but was happy to extend *pet* coverage? Weird, right? When that policy was spotlighted by gay activists in the summer of 2004, Home Depot quickly switched gears and offered partner insurance (in addition to pet coverage, of course). But at least three other Fortune 500 companies today still favor pets over people.[29]

Moving to the Mainstream

Corporate tone deafness can be the result of many things.

It can result from stuck-in-the mud leadership. It can result from a particular corporate context—geographic, social, or whatever—that simply takes some things off the table. Conversely, some contexts put things *on* the table. Why did the *Village Voice* embrace domestic partner benefits first? Easy: because it was in Greenwich Village, where all sorts of interesting things are possible. Why was Berkeley second? Because Berkeley was Berkeley, and no place else in the world is quite like Berkeley.

Corporate tone deafness can also be the result of a particular function's being too removed from the corporate fast track. The fact is, corporate hotshots don't tend to congregate in the human resources area. Corporate hotshots head into finance, strategy, or sales, or they go out and run an operating unit. The sad truth is that the only time these folks think about employee benefits is when benefits get too expensive. Then the guys in the executive offices wake up to things like health plans, co-pays, and partner benefits, they call an off-site meeting, they ring bells and blow whistles, and then they go looking for a new managed-care provider.

But that's not good enough. That's the thinking that got us where we are today. As Harvard's Professor Herzlinger puts it:

> If you are buying steel for a car company, you are right in the main part of the company. If you are buying health insurance, organizationally you are off to the sidelines. So the revolution in health care will have to come from the CEOs.[30]

Yes, exactly: *it's going to take a CEO.* And also an aroused populace and some courageous legislators—at both the federal and state levels—who are willing to back that "revolution" with appropriate laws and tax policies.

10

THE CEO CHECKLIST

What takes a CEO?

And why do we need CEOs, anyway?

CEOs became necessary in the later nineteenth century, when businesses got too large and complicated to be run by their entrepreneurial founders. The new breed of manager—the professional manager—was, in essence, a hired gun. He took orders from the owners, hired other guys like himself to help run and grow the business, and tried to stay out of the newspapers.

This proved to be a durable model. The chief executive officers throughout much of the twentieth century—let's say, until well into the post–World War II decades—were less like pop stars and more like very well paid bus drivers. They weren't flamboyant, but if they were good at their jobs, they got you where you wanted to go. Their formal title was "president." True, they were the "chief executive officers" of their organizations, but rarely did they use that particular title. It was too obvious.

Starting late in the second half of the twentieth century, a good number of the bus drivers climbed down off their buses and started sashaying around like pop stars. They were now "chief executive officers," which is only one rung down from "Exalted Vizier." As noted earlier, this development can be arbitrarily dated to July

1986, the publication date of Lee Iacocca's self-aggrandizing auto-biography, titled—what else?—*Iacocca*. It was not a good day for management.

There's one more player we have to put on the examining table before we can answer the two questions posed above. That player is the corporation itself.

THE ARTIFICIAL PERSON

The corporation was invented, way back when, with an eye toward sharing and mitigating risk. The idea was that investors would put their money into an entity that was once removed from themselves, and if anything went terribly wrong afterward, the investors couldn't be pursued individually for the sins, debts, or other fail-ures of the corporation. This shield (and, of course, the promise of huge returns) helped assemble the increasingly large pools of capi-tal that were needed to launch enterprises.

Society first tolerated and then encouraged the formation of corporations, because corporations got things done. Corporations built canals, railroads, and bridges across America's wide rivers. At the same time, however, society put tight constraints on corpora-tions. Simply put, we didn't trust them. "I hope we shall crush in its birth the aristocracy of our moneyed corporations," wrote Thomas Jefferson in 1816, "which dare already to challenge our govern-ment to a trial of strength and bid defiance to the laws of our country."[1]

In the early days of the Republic, most corporate charters were time-limited: after a preset period of time, the corporation died a natural death. While they were alive, corporations were only per-mitted to do what their charters explicitly sanctioned. They couldn't make political contributions or lobby government offi-cials. They couldn't own stock in other corporations (in fact, they couldn't own *anything* that didn't directly relate to the business at hand). And perhaps most important, corporations in the newly formed United States of America could be chartered only by legis-latures and not by kings, governors, or other potentates. The peo-ple wanted to tightly control the corporate beast.

Then came the first of two fateful Supreme Court decisions. In 1819, only three years after Jefferson fretted aloud about the power of "moneyed corporations," the Court ruled that New Hampshire didn't have the right to revoke the charter of Dartmouth College, granted by King George III in 1769. (The New Hampshire legislature wasn't hostile to Dartmouth per se, but they were determined to cleanse it of its royalist origins.) The high court's decision was correctly interpreted by the states as a frontal assault on their rights. Nineteen states subsequently rewrote their constitutions to give themselves the authority to revoke corporate charters.

The second fateful Supreme Court ruling came in 1886, in the case of *Santa Clara County v. Southern Pacific Railroad Company.* Santa Clara County in California had been taxing Southern Pacific's lands and rights-of-way, and for six years the railroad had refused to pay those taxes. The Southern Pacific's lawyers staked out the odd defense that their client was a "person" under the terms of the Fourteenth Amendment to the Constitution—the equal protection amendment—and therefore should not be subject to the whims of a county, which (the lawyers claimed) was discriminating against the Southern Pacific through its allegedly unequal tax system. *All persons are equal before the law,* the railroad lawyers argued.[2] *Think of Southern Pacific as, say, a somewhat noisy, smoky, and outsized next-door neighbor.*

Inexplicably, the Court bought this argument. In an offhanded sort of way, the Court ruled that corporations were indeed persons:

> The court does not wish to hear argument on the question whether the provision in the Fourteenth Amendment to the Constitution, which forbids a State to deny to any person within its jurisdiction the equal protection of the laws, applied to these corporations. We are all of opinion that it does.[3]

Suddenly, the constitutional amendment that was originally passed to ban slavery was now being used to create artificial persons. This was particularly perverse, given that this new category of "person" was owned outright by other people, which was exactly what the Fourteenth Amendment was intended to prevent. And these artificial persons weren't just ordinary people like you and me. They were immortal and powerful and soulless.

Do you see our two trend lines converging? On the one hand, you've got court-sanctioned, immortal corporations that don't have to worry about meeting their Maker, and on the other hand, you've got samurai pop-star CEOs looking to grab the microphone, puff themselves up, and feather their own nests. And these developments are compounded today in those now highly concentrated industries and media empires we looked at in earlier chapters, which are taking full advantage of deregulation to further destroy competition, drive down wages, and even subvert our democracy.

So the question we have to ask is, *Where are the moral compasses, and who's in charge of reading them?*

The CEO checklist

You can anticipate the answer: it takes a CEO.

But not just any kind of CEO. Not the kinds of CEOs we came across in our brief tours of Sinclair Broadcast, WorldCom, Enron, and Wal-Mart. No, it's going to take a CEO with a very special set of characteristics. You've already encountered all of these characteristics, at least implicitly, in previous chapters. Here, I'll summarize them in a CEO checklist.

Ideally, the checklist would be addressed to the CEO: *Here are nineteen things that you, the current or prospective CEO, should describe and define as you go about your business.* But there are only a couple of thousand people in that potential audience, and most of them don't listen to me anyway. So let's look at the checklist from the point of view of a prospective employee—one who's trying to decide whether this particular CEO and company are worthy of his or her best efforts, and therefore worth signing on with.

Perhaps this approach seems odd, especially after all the recent years of recession and relatively jobless recovery. Then there's the whole challenge of outsourcing and offshoring. *I'm lucky to come up with any kind of job,* you may be thinking. *What the heck are you talking about, asking if this company is "worth signing on with"?*

Yes, choices have narrowed in recent years. And yes, when people come under economic pressure, they sometimes make choices that they wouldn't make otherwise. Think of all those people who resent the way they're treated by Wal-Mart but work there because they have no other choice—at least for now.

But as much as possible, we have to look past the frustrations, even the miseries, of the moment to chart longer-term courses. In Chapter 6, I quoted Max DePree, the visionary former CEO of Herman Miller. DePree is fond of saying that all employees are volunteers. What does he mean? He means that people voluntarily join an organization and lend their skills and personal credibility to it because on some level *they believe in that organization.* And their belief helps make the organization, and its CEO, successful.

So no, the CEO isn't the be-all and end-all of a company. Far from it. But just as the principal sets the tone in the school, the minister sets the tone in the church, and the captain sets the tone on the ship, so the CEO sets the tone in the company. When you go shopping for a place to commit your time, energy, and loyalty, look to the top first. And ask yourself whether the man or woman you see there has the following characteristics:

Bright, well educated, and well-informed?

Today, more than ever, the leader of a company has to be outward-looking and forward-looking. He has to have both a broad perspective and a deep reservoir of knowledge about the company and its competitors. Listen to him talk or, less reliably, read what he has written. (When it comes to writing, he may simply have good speechwriters at work.) Is this someone who can guess where the competition is going and leapfrog over those competitors? How smart is he, anyway? Where did he go to school? Is he active in the lives of those institutions?

An inquiring mind?

An extension of the above. Smarts and education aren't worth much if the CEO doesn't apply them. Again, the standards are *broad* and *deep*. What kinds of scouting parties does this CEO send out? When confronted with a business puzzle, how deeply does she dig down to get the answer? How does she react when she finally gets the answer? If she's delighted, that's a very good sign.

What does she read? Whom does she quote? Does she ever attend symposia, colloquia, or other gatherings that aren't directly related to the conduct of the business? Does she ever make speeches? Why, and to whom?

Articulate?

A leader can't lead without being able to articulate the vision. This has two main components: 1) the ability to think straight, and 2) the ability to express those thoughts in ways that speak directly to the crowd he is addressing. Good body language, good timing, knowing how to use a microphone, a pleasant speaking voice: all of these are helpful, of course. But there's a deeper level of articulation—one that's hard to describe, but you sure know it when you hear it. It comes from the person who gives his brain and his heart equal access to his tongue, so that what he expresses comes out both pointed and passionate.

Exceptionally hardworking?

Thomas Edison is some people's candidate for ultimate CEO. You've surely heard him quoted to the effect that genius is 10 percent inspiration and 90 percent perspiration. Well, so's leadership. You've simply got to put in the hours: there's no other way to get the job done and inspire others to also give their utmost. A great CEO earns his or her pay, and then some—assuming, of course, that the pay scale is in touch with reality.

As a subset of this point, I'd suggest that the CEO needs to be in reasonably good physical shape. I've always believed that physical exercise, done right, creates more energy than it consumes. How does your CEO keep his or her batteries charged?

Honest and ethical?

Asking that a leader be honest and ethical sounds like a call for motherhood and apple pie, right? Maybe so, but it still bears repeating. An organization simply can't thrive under a leader who doesn't have a really good sense of what's right, period. A fish rots from the head, as they say. Harley-Davidson's Rich Teerlink phrased it this way:

> CEOs are the "keepers of the values" of their organization, at least until those values become a real, engrained, embedded part of the organization's members. With or without a context of change, but especially in a context of change, the CEO must act as the organizational role model. A single beacon alone is not sufficient illumination, of course, but the absence of this one beacon can undercut all others.[4]

And just to complicate things a little bit, a great leader also has a clear sense of what *appears* to be right. In other words, not only does she instantly rule out bad behavior, but she also rules out behaviors that might be misconstrued to her disadvantage or to the disadvantage of the company.

Appearance questions aren't always cut-and-dried. What's cosmetically OK in one industry may not be in another. And the rules are definitely different in the public and private sectors. Not too long ago, there was a governor of Massachusetts, Jane Swift, whose home was in the far western part of the state, something like 150 miles from the state house in Boston. She was the mother of young children. Getting out of Boston via the Mass Pike on a Thanksgiving weekend, as most people who've tried it will agree, is an ugly experience. So in November 1999, with a young child at home who was sick and in need of mothering, the governor hooked a ride home in a state police helicopter.[5] Dishonest or unethical? Not really. Likely to reflect badly on her and rile up the taxpayers? You bet. (It did.)

"The tone is set at the top," commented Bill Donaldson, until just recently the Chairman of the SEC. "You must have an internal code of ethics that goes beyond the letter of the law to also encompass the spirit of the law."[6] Exactly.

Demonstrates a sense of fairness and fair play?

Have you spent time with any young children recently? Youngsters have an exquisite, almost paralyzing sense of fairness. They can spend more time making up the rules and enforcing the rules than they spend actually playing the game.

No, you don't want *exactly* that quality in your CEO. On the other hand, a strong sense of what's fair, and also the capacity for moral outrage when the rules are flouted, are necessary qualities in a leader.

Lives life with grace?

A CEO needs to be comfortable with himself and with the world. He needs to be able to forgive other people and forgive himself. He needs to have grace.

Grace is a fine old word, with religious roots. In that context, it denotes both God's love for humankind and the condition of being free of sin (in a "state of grace"). In a more secular sense, according to my word-processing program, it denotes "dignified, polite, and decent behavior," or "a capacity to tolerate, accommodate, or forgive people."

Think of someone you know who conducts himself with grace. Did you conjure up an image of someone who is *physically* graceful, like a dancer, a figure skater, or some other kind of athlete? If so, now think instead of an individual who *lives* graciously—with fairness, elegance, decency, and tolerance. Humor and sensitivity enter into the picture here too. Again, it's hard to describe, but we all know grace when we see it. And we all miss it when we *don't* see it.

Loves people?

Businesses are all about people. Patents expire. Technologies get overtaken. Mines play out. But all of the time, you've gotta love people, period.

Hates bigotry?

If business is all about people, then no business can afford to belittle, sabotage, or reject whole classes of people. Think of all the energy that gets wasted on drawing lines between group 1 and group 2, with group 1 telling group 2 that because of the way they are, they can't cross that line.

Two of the strangest words in the English language are *quadroon* and *octoroon*—relics of the time, now mostly behind us, when we used to keep track of how "black" somebody was. How long will it be before we stop throwing up barriers in front of people who are gay or handicapped or otherwise out of the societal mainstream? Not much longer, I hope. Because we don't have time for that kind of inhumanity and nonsense.

Shows courage?

A CEO has to demonstrate several kinds of courage. There's the dramatic, high-visibility kind of courage that occasionally makes its way into magazine articles or TV news features—the courage that's required for bet-the-company kinds of decisions, where if you make the wrong call, thousands of families get wiped out.

There's also the kind of courage it takes to admit you've made a bonehead mistake that has hurt the company, and which you're now determined to fix. Take Bill Gates's celebrated turnaround on the internet. Belatedly, Gates realized that the internet wasn't a sideshow to the game; it *was* the game. He ate crow, and he fought and bought his way back into that game.

And finally, there's the kind of courage it takes to get out of bed in the morning. Speaking from personal experience, there are times when it feels as if you're looking down the darkest of dark holes and there's no way out—and *still* you have to find a way out. All those people you are responsible for, and who, you hope, respect you, are counting on you.

Takes (smart) risks?

In your CEO, you want a man or woman who is eager to lead the charge. But you *don't* want Pickett's Charge or the Charge of the Light Brigade. You sure don't want some French guy standing on a nearby hilltop shaking his head and saying, *"C'est magnifique, mais ce n'est pas le guerre."* ("Great theater, Lord Cardigan, but really bad business.")

Smart risk-taking is about being as well-informed and well-advised as possible. And it is also about controlling risks that are simply too high. For example, you can share risks with other enterprises or stage the risks so that, if necessary, you have multiple opportunities to disengage from what might turn out to be a bad initial decision.

Makes tough decisions in a timely way?

Once the leader has summoned up her courage and she's gotten the odds as much in her favor as they're going to get, she has to pull the trigger.

Southwest Airlines's Herb Kelleher once talked about the challenges of acting upon incomplete information:

> You can never obtain perfect knowledge. . . . If you can't have perfect knowledge, you're taking a risk, but you have to be prepared to take those risks. You have to be prepared to make those judgments. And you have to be prepared to move ahead. And you have to be prepared to correct quickly any mistakes that you might make—quickly—not have mistakes that you're so egotistical about . . . that you say, "Oh, my lord, I can't do anything about this, because it'll admit I was wrong." You know what I mean: say, "Well, I was wrong. I've got to correct it, instantaneously."[7]

Within reason, people in organizations are willing to tolerate a few missteps, provided that their leader moves quickly in what looks like a sensible direction. Think back to the example of Franklin Roosevelt, who took over as president at what was arguably one of the most frightening junctures in U.S. history. He had no strong ideas about how to get the country out of the mess it was in, but he made tough calls quickly—and undid them when they didn't work. People saw courage in his actions, with *actions* being the key word.

Acts on conviction?

Remember how Johnson & Johnson's Jim Burke pulled Tylenol off the shelves in response to poisonings caused by product tampering. People outside the company were astonished at his willingness to tackle the issue head-on—even at the risk of killing his vitally lucrative brand. There surely were people inside the company who argued for stalling and looking for another way out. No matter: Burke acted on conviction.

People want to know that their leader has something at his or her core. They want to know that when the foul-weather winds start to blow, the CEO has something reliable inside to fall back on. His or her personal rudder becomes the organizational rudder. It prevents foundering. It prevents drift. It stays the course.

Demonstrates patience—up to a point?

Good leaders are teachers, and good teachers are patient. They don't expect people to break old habits overnight or to master difficult things perfectly the first time out. They cut some slack, when slack is needed.

But good leaders also know when to swap out the carrot for the stick. They know when to call a time-out and change the play—or the players.

And finally, they also know when, and how, to ease someone out of a position that's terminally uncomfortable, without demoralizing that person and his or her coworkers. Back in August 2004, HP's CEO Carly Fiorina took exactly the opposite tack. She singled out three of her executives by name, and—in front of all the world—fired them for allegedly causing her company to miss the unrealistic targets that she herself was responsible for setting. This is management by blame shifting, humiliation, and public execution, and it never works.

Spots talent (and keeps on looking)?

The CEO has to have the capacity to find people who are better than the ones the organization has today. (How else will the place get better?) Then, having bet on an individual, the CEO has to be willing to track the success of that commitment and later understand why it was a good (or bad) choice. If the person hired isn't doing as well as expected, how do we interpret that? Was the job description not quite right? Was the individual oversold to us, or did we overbuy? Has something in the environment changed that has turned a good fit into a bad one?

Spotting talent is both a gift and a skill—and therefore a capacity that's hard to cultivate. So my unsolicited advice to the CEO who doesn't have this gift is to *find somebody who does*—and in a hurry. Surround yourself with good people who can find and nurture good people. Businesses are all about people.

Delegates without second-guessing?

Somewhere along the line, most of us have had a boss who was a pseudodelegator—an individual who either pretends to let go of the reins but actually keeps them tightly gathered up, or lets go of the reins, has second thoughts, and then kneecaps the horse just when it starts moving out of the gate.

This is organizational poison. Delegation is like pregnancy: either it's happening, or it's not happening. Nothing destroys motivation or employee self-confidence like pseudodelegation.

A good CEO lets his or her people make just about any kind of honest mistake once.

But not the same mistake *twice,* of course—nor careless ones.

Acknowledges multiple constituencies and responsibilities?

History seems to have lost sight of Reginald H. Jones, who preceded Jack Welch as chairman and CEO of General Electric. That's a mistake; he was an outstanding corporate leader.[8] When Jones became CEO in 1972, he made memorable speeches to both the Business Roundtable and the National Press Club. In those agenda-setting remarks, he said that henceforth he would view his responsibilities as being evenly split among the company and its employees, American industry, and the nation.

Let's label these categories slightly. Let's call out shareholders as an explicit stakeholder—a constituency that Jones implicitly included under his "company" umbrella—and also call out community explicitly. (It turns out that GE, up to and during Jones's era, would have benefited from paying a little more attention to some of those communities and the rivers that ran through them.) Few of us ever get to a company as big as GE, but when you get up where the air gets thin, at the very top of the corporate hierarchy, you definitely have to consider the nation as one of your stakeholders. Today, more than ever, our nation needs CEO statesmen, and the gifted and caring Reg Jones was certainly one of the best ever.

Take another example. When Landmark Communications, which conceived and launched the Weather Channel, began contemplating a plan to take its fabulously successful weather.com public, chairman Frank Batten worried aloud about what would happen to the company's *future* employees:

> There was one telling question to which I never got a satisfactory answer: "What does the *next* generation of good people at weather.com get, after the value of the company has been handed out to this generation?" As long as I lacked a good answer to that question, I felt an IPO would be hard to justify.[9]

Again, good thinking, and highly responsible. As a CEO, you succeed in the long run by defining your universe of stakeholders broadly. When you do, you arrive at better solutions, by anyone's definition you are fairer, and you avoid unnecessary battles (and approach the necessary ones better prepared).

Knows where the buck really stops?

One last little history lesson: in poker, the person whose turn it is to deal is indicated by a marker. If that person chooses not to deal, he or she passes the marker to the next player. Back in frontier days, this marker often took the form of a knife with a handle that was made of buck horn. So the person who didn't want to deal "passed the buck" on to the next player.[10]

Harry Truman liked nothing better than a good game of poker—preferably eight-handed, and with plenty of cigars available.[11] He certainly knew the origin of "passing the buck." So when a plaque arrived at the White House in October 1945 engraved with "The Buck Stops Here," Truman happily displayed it on his desk. And when he made his farewell address to the nation in January 1953, he underscored the point for all to hear. "The President—whoever he is—has to decide," Truman said. "He can't pass the buck to anybody. No one else can do the deciding for him. That's his job."[12]

The same is true for the CEO. Everyone else can weigh in; no one else can do the deciding.

Tolerates loneliness?

Perhaps this sounds a little self-indulgent: *Woe is me! All this power and money, and nobody to call my friend.*

But the truth is that great responsibility is a great isolator. The CEO doesn't have much of a peer group. He has outgrown or outlived his mentors. With individuals and groups competing for his attention and approval, he can't afford to oversocialize or to seem partial. He has to make decisions that are bound to make some people unhappy.

And viewed from the other side of the fence, people are intimidated. They tend to get a little stiff and tongue-tied around the CEO. They dress up: themselves and their workplaces. Someone once said that the Queen of England must think that all the world smells of fresh paint. CEOs can identify with that.

For many, this isolation turns out to be one of the great challenges. CEOs tend to love people. And yet, they have to both put up fences and respect the fences that other people put up. They have to be willing to be lonely.

IN THE END, IT TAKES A CEO

So there you have it: nineteen things you need to look for in your next CEO. Or, if you are already sitting in the corner office or think you're clearly on your way there, nineteen things you need to keep in the front of your brain.

Let me anticipate and try to head off two possible criticisms.

The first might be that *few people in the world meet all these criteria.* True enough. But CEOs are by definition a rare breed, and truly great CEOs are even rarer. Every CEO needs to cultivate each of these traits and needs to strive every day to manifest and to grow into them. While perfection every day isn't possible, there must be the desire every day to go nineteen for nineteen—and also the willingness to look and listen for signals that you're coming up short in some department. And finally, of course, there's the substantial challenge of improving something in yourself, or compensating for a shortcoming if you can't figure out a way to fix it.

The second criticism might be that *the checklist focuses too much on top-down leadership*. In other words, by concentrating on the CEO, the checklist actually exacerbates the CEO-as-samurai-pop-star problem. Both Herman Miller's Max DePree and Harley's Rich Teerlink, mentioned earlier, would likely disagree. The simple fact is that great followership is just as important as great leadership—probably even more important. Consider where management guru Peter Senge starts, and winds up, on this particular point:

> So long as we cling to the notion that "leader" means top manager and strong leadership means powerful executives, the perpetual search for the hero CEO will continue. Indeed, worshipping the cult of the hero-leader may be the primary cause for maintaining change-averse institutions. An alternative is to re-establish an older notion of a leader as someone who "steps ahead," who has the courage, capability, and credibility to inspire change at many levels.[13]

Well said. Sometimes the best new idea is an "older notion." Nonetheless, the nineteen characteristics outlined above are the right prescription for stepping ahead—and, just as important, for helping other people step ahead with you.

Politicians of all stripes are fond of saying that "America's best days are still ahead of her," or words to that effect. Part of me—my heart, I think—dearly wants to agree with that. Like lots of Americans, I'm an incorrigible optimist. When someone appeals to my optimistic streak, I tend to respond. *Our best days are still ahead of us? Sounds good to me!*

The problem is that getting to those best days isn't going to happen automatically. It's not like a train rolling downhill into Station Paradise: sit back and enjoy the ride, America. Getting to the right place—whether as a person, a CEO, a company, or a society—takes smarts, courage, vision, sacrifice, persistence, grace, and timing.

Arthur Levitt recently wrote in the *Wall Street Journal* that the "imperial CEO is no more."[14] I wish I believed that. Changing entrenched bad habits—intellectual, philosophical, moral—takes a lot of work.

It takes contributions from lots of players. It takes politicians who are willing to risk short-term disapproval in return for long-term societal gain. It takes regulators who—despite political pressure—can draw tight lines around bad behavior and at the same time open new doors to good behavior. It takes judges who stand up for hard-won rights and freedom, which, too often today, are being eroded. It takes consumers who are willing to pay a few pennies more for a given good or service in order to save jobs for others. It takes boards of directors who collectively ride herd on the corporate beasts, thereby helping to make them truly responsible agents of progress.

And, of course, it takes a CEO.

NOTES

1: The Problem, and How We Got There

1. Janny Scott, "Nearly Half of Black Men Found Jobless," *New York Times*, 2/28/04.
2. Statistics from *Health Insurance Coverage in America*, Kaiser Commission on Medicaid and the Uninsured, December 2003.
3. "Janet Bares Breast During Dinner Hour," at www.newsandentertainment.com/janet_jackson_superbowl.html.
4. "Citigroup Agrees to a Settlement over WorldCom," in *New York Times*, online edition, 5/11/04.
5. www.pbs.org/wgbh/pages/frontlines/shows/wallstreet/wcom/players.html.
6. To settle charges that it slanted research to support huge investment-banking fees, Citigroup agreed to pay $400 million.
7. From "Fiscal Survey of States: June 2005," p. 18, www.nasbo.org/Publications/fiscalsurvey/fsspring2005.pdf. The figures are actual expenditures for 2001—a little outdated, but you get the idea.
8. "Calories Still Count," www.healthstatus.com/calories_count.html, citing an unnamed study from the National Institutes of Health.
9. From the Web site of the federally sponsored International Trade Association, www.ita.doc.gov/td/auto/cafe.html.
10. Robert D. Putnam, *Bowling Alone* (New York: Simon & Schuster, 2000). See page 187, and surrounding pages, for the full catalog of contributing factors.
11. Time Warner's Web site, perhaps revised since Levin's departure in 2002, proudly proclaims that "we work to improve our communi-

ties—taking pride in serving the public interest as well as the interests of our shareholders." www.timewarnercable.com/corporate/aboutus/ourvision.html (accessed 7/28/05). I note in passing that Levin's decision to sell Time Warner to AOL resulted in a 75 percent decline in the value of the combined company's stock: not exactly a triumph of shareholder-wealth maximization.

12. "Senators Propose Banning Extreme-Fighting Matches," *Olympian,* 1/21/04, www.theolympian.com/home/specialsections/Legislature/20040121/18250.shtml.

2: The Few. The Proud. The Brave.

1. "Tough at the Top," *Economist,* 10/25/03, pp. 3–22.
2. The original Hippocratic oath is more complicated: it prohibits all sorts of practices, including various kinds of "mischief" (such as engaging in sexual relations with either male or female patients, free or slave). Modern versions are more concise.
3. Professor Harrell retired years ago and died in the spring of 2002, but his survey was continued by other faculty members. Harrell conducted a number of interesting studies of various SBS student cohorts. Among his findings: outgoing, gregarious grads tended to be more successful professionally than "nerds," and marriage tended to hurt women's careers while helping men's careers. See his obituary at www.gsb.stanford.edu/news/harrell_obituary.html.
4. David Lieberman, "This American Dream Turned into Nightmare," *USA Today,* 7/9/04.
5. Mark Maremont and Laurie P. Cohen, "Tyco Spent Millions for the Benefit of Kozlowski, Its Former CEO," Mark Maremont, Laurie P. Cohen, *Wall Street Journal,* 8/7/02. See also *Wall Street Journal Online,* 8/7/02, at www.happinessonline.org/InfectiousGreed/p1.htm.
6. Ken Moritsugu, "Enron Retirees Tell How They Got Wiped Out," *Detroit Free Press,* 12/19/01, www.freep.com/money/business/enron19_20011219.htm.
7. The quote is from *New York Times Magazine,* 6/13/04. I feel compelled to refer to Watkins as the "so-called" Enron whistle-blower because she didn't actually go very far with her whistle-blowing, restricting her corporate critique to an (admittedly blistering) e-mail to Lay. For the full text of that e-mail, see www.itmweb.com/f012002.htm.
8. www.economist.com/displaystory.cfm?story_id=S%27%2980%28QA%2B%20%21P%23T%0A.

3: Deregulation, Concentration, and Worm Juice

1. Dean Booth's article appeared in the July 1971 issue of *Transportation Law Journal*. I found this citation in Paul Craig Roberts, "Did Airline Deregulation Fail?" at www.wdare.com/roberts/airlines.htm.

2. For an excellent summary of airline deregulation, see Jonathan Byrnes, "Airline Deregulation: Lessons for Telecom," in *Working Knowledge*, a Harvard Business School publication, at http://hbswk .hbs.edu/item.jhtml?id=4173&t=dispatch (accessed: 7/28/05).

3. See Roberts, "Did Airline Deregulation Fail?"

4. The July 2002 issue of *Consumer Reports* focused on the impact of deregulation on consumers. Its conclusions were almost entirely negative.

5. Robert Kuttner, "Useless Airways," *Prospect,* 9/9/02, www.prospect .org/V13/16/kuttner-r.html. Since the time of Kuttner's article, other airlines have entered this market.

6. Bev Desjarlais, "NDP Minority Report on the Restructuring of Canada's Airline Industry: Modern Regulation in the National Interest," www.parl.gc.ca/InfoComDoc/36/2/TRAN/Studies/Reports/, accessed 7/23/04.

7. All of these dreadful conversations are available in PDF form at the *Houston Chronicle* Web site, www.houstonchronicle.com. On the same topic, see the interesting article by Jonathan Peterson, "Enron Tapes Shed Light on Ploys in California," 6/22/04, www.chron .com/cs/CDA/ssistory.mpl/business/2577156.

8. April Witt and Peter Behr, "The Fall of Enron—Losses, Conflict Threaten Survival," *Washington Post,* 7/31/02.

9. John T. Landry and Jeffrey L. Cruikshank, *From the Rivers: The Origins and Growth of the New England Electric System,* (Westborough, MA: NEES, 1996), p. vii.

10. See "Krugman on Electricity Regulation: The Road to Ruin," www .Bluebus.org/archives/000508.php.

11. From "U.S.–Canada Power System Outage Task Force, August 14th Blackout: Causes and Recommendations," p. 143, www.ferc.gov/ press-room/press-releases.asp.

12. Floyd Norris, "Making a Mockery of Media Concentration Rules," *New York Times,* 11/21/03.

13. See, for example, Jennifer S. Lee, "Musicians Protesting Monopoly in Media," *New York Times,* 12/18/03, www.mediaaccess.org/ program/diversity/MusiciansProtestMonopoly.htm.

14. Adam Buckman, "Heidi 'ho,' " *New York Post,* 3/10/04.

15. Robert Bianco, "There's Nothing Beautiful About 'The Swan,' " *USA Today,* 4/12/04.

16. Dennis Hunt, " 'Fear Factor' Knows How to Survive," *USA Today,* 11/4/03.

17. Brooks Barnes, "For 'Fear Factor,' Getting Boring Is the Real Danger," *Wall Street Journal*, 4/29/04.
18. From American Academy of Pediatrics, "Sexuality, Conception, and the Media," quoted in "Sex-Ed Night School," *New York Times*, 11/16/03.
19. Quoted in Roberts, "Did Airline Deregulation Fail?"
20. Brooks Boliek, "DeLay, Daschle Pushing for Fines," *Hollywood Reporter*, 3/3/04.
21. See "Menomonie Will Lose Greyhound Service," *Dunn County News*, www.dunnconnect.com/articles/2004/06/30/news/news02.txt.
22. Charles Edward Scott Jr., "Lamers Won't Pick Up Old Greyhound Routes," *Wausau Daily Herald*, 7/10/04, www.wausaudailyherald.com/wdhlocal/280939058790588.shtml.
23. Peyton L. Wynns, "The Limits of Economic Regulation: The U.S. Experience," June 2004, working paper, p. 8, available online through a link at http://hraunfoss.fcc.gov/edocs_public/attachmatch/DOC-248597A1.pdf.
24. Kyle Gearhart, "CWA Eyes Expansion in Long Run," *Wausau Daily Herald*, 2/5/04, www.wausaudailyherald.com/wdhbusiness/291913010972638.shtml.

4: Putting Democracy on the Block

1. Julia Angwin, "Sinclair Tells Eight Stations Not to Air 'Nightline' Special," *Wall Street Journal*, 4/30/04.
2. "Statement of Sinclair Broadcast Group," www.newscentral.tv/station/statement.shtml.
3. Paul Schmeizer, "The Death of Local News," on *Alternet*, www.alternet.org/story/15718.
4. From the company's Web site, www.sbgi.net/about/history.shtml.
5. Statistics from "McCain Rebukes Sinclair 'Nightline' Decision," www.cnn.com/2004/SHOWBIZ/TV/04/29/abc.nightline/.
6. See the company profile at *Yahoo! Finance*, biz.yahoo.com/ic/44/44667.html.
7. Angwin, "Sinclair Tells Eight Stations."
8. From the company's Web site, www.sbgi.net/business/news.shtml.
9. From McCain's Web site, www.mccain.senate.gov/index.cfm?fuseaction=Newscenter.ViewPressRelease&Content_id=1276.
10. "McCain Rebukes Sinclair 'Nightline' Decision."
11. This is how both Julian Sinclair Smith and Ted Turner, among others, got into the TV field. For an interesting personal perspective on these issues, see Turner's article "My Beef with Big Media," *Washington*

Monthly, April 2004, www.washingtonmonthly.com/features/2004/0407.turner.html. I have drawn upon this article, among others, for my historical summary.

12. "Testimony of Gene Kimmelman, Senior Director for Advocacy and Public Policy, Consumers Union, before the Antitrust, Competition Policy and Consumer Rights Subcommittee of the Senate Judiciary Committee on News Corp./DirecTV Merger, June 18, 2003," www.consumersunion.org.

13. Turner, "My Beef with Big Media."

14. "Remarks, FCC Commissioner Michael J. Copps, Columbia Law School Forum on Media Ownership, January 16, 2003," www.fcc.gov. See also Chairman Powell's remarks at the same forum.

15. Brent Staples, "The Trouble with Corporate Radio: The Day the Protest Music Died," www.nytimes.com/2003/02/20/opinion/20THU4.html.

16. "Does Ownership Matter in Local Television News?" www.journalism.org/resources/research/reports/ownership/default.asp.

17. "McCain Bill Diversifies Ownership in Telecommunications Industry," mccain.senate.gov/index.cfm?fuseaction=Newscenter.ViewPressRelease&Content_id=722.

18. Staples, "The Trouble with Corporate Radio."

19. From "McCain Rebukes Sinclair 'Nightline' Decision."

20. I owe a debt of gratitude to the *Columbia Journalism Review* for assembling this monstrous list, which can be viewed in its entirety—for example, including radio station call letters by city—at www.cjr.org/tools/owners/disney.asp.

21. "Disney Is Blocking Distribution of Film That Criticizes Bush," *New York Times,* 5/5/04.

22. Ibid.

23. These facts come from "House of Bush, House of Mickey," at the Center for American Progress's Web site, www.reclaimthemedia.org/stories.php?story=04/05/07/2761670.

24. "Disney Is Blocking Distribution."

25. Michael Moore, "Disney Has Blocked Distribution of My New Film," www.michaelmoore.com/words/message/index.php?messageDate=2004-05-04.

26. "Disney's Craven Behavior," *New York Times,* 5/6/04.

27. www.boxofficemojo.com/movies/?id=fahrenheit911.htm.

28. Philip Shenon, "Will Michael Moore's Facts Check Out?" *New York Times,* 6/20/04.

29. Denis Hamill, "Moore's Message Delivered, Big-time," *New York Daily News,* 6/29/04.

30. Turner, "My Beef with Big Media."

31. 274 U.S. 357 (1927).

5: CEO Compensation: What's Wrong, What's Right

1. Mark Maremont and Laurie P. Cohen, "Tyco Spent Millions for the Benefit of Kozlowski, Its Former CEO," *Wall Street Journal Online,* 8/7/02, www.happinessonline.org/InfectiousGreed/p1.htm.

2. "Tyco Accountant Testifies About Expenses," *Wall Street Journal,* 11/20/03.

3. Bonuses more or less fell off the table, as the three other kinds of compensation became outlandishly outsized. Bonuses—which, if well defined, have a certain obvious *rightness* to them—have started to make a quiet comeback in recent years.

4. This excerpt, as well as the "62 times" statistic, are from "Executive Compensation: Summary Observations on a Workshop Held at Harvard Business School on October 10, 2002," by HBS professors Brian J. Hall and Thomas Piper, www.cglv.hbs.edu/workshops/exec-comp.html. This Web site, which includes other papers and presentations, provides an excellent grounding in the larger issues of corporate governance, leadership, and values.

5. Brian Morrissey, "Executive Pay 2000: An Embarrassment of Riches," www.inequality.org/ceopay20002.html. To be precise, in this context Kozlowski was talking about his options, but I think it's easy to extend this way of thinking to the realm of boodle.

6. See James Surowiecki, "Blame Iacocca," slate.msn.com/toolbar .aspx?action=print&id=2068448. And, of course, read Collins's book, if you haven't already.

7. I've always had trouble with this guy. I remember clearly when, in 1984, he called air bags a solution that was worse than the problem. Four years later, he put them into his Chryslers and claimed that he had *always* been all about safety. Learning on the job? Or historical revisionism?

8. Statistics from Morrissey, "Executive Pay 2000."

9. Instead of showing growth through acquisitions—a path that doesn't necessarily show brilliant leadership that might possibly be worth a billion a year—CA's leaders allegedly wanted to show organic, internally derived growth. Alex Berenson, "Computer Associates May Face S.E.C. Action," *New York Times,* 1/13/04.

10. Ibid.

11. Ian Lynch, "Computer Associates Faces SEC Charges," 1/13/04, www.vnunet.com/news/1152003.

12. "Kumar to Leave Computer Associates," Computer Associates Web site press file, www3.ca.com/press/PressReleases.asp?CID=59939.

13. "Ex-CEO Gave Up Stock and Options," *New York Times,* 7/30/04.

14. "CA Reports Major Stockholder Supports Board Opposition of Shareholder Proposal," Computer Associates Web site press file, www3.ca.com/press/PressReleases.asp?CID=61850.

15. Hall and Piper, "Executive Compensation."
16. Paul Krugman, "Executives Gone Wild," book review, *New York Times Book Review*, 2/8/04, p. 9. The factoid, cited in Krugman's review, comes from Roger Lowenstein's *Origins of the Crash* (New York: Penguin, 2004).
17. Scott DeCarlo, "The Best and Worst Bosses," *Forbes*, 5/10/04, www.forbes.com/free_forbes/2004/0510/108.html?partner=yahoo &referrer=.
18. Dean Baker and Arcon Fung, "How to Tame CEO Compensation," *Harvard Business School Working Knowledge*, hbswk.edu/item .jhtml?id=2917&t=outsourcing.
19. Ibid.
20. Jeffrey L. Cruikshank and Clark Malcolm, *Herman Miller, Inc.: Buildings and Beliefs* (Washington, D.C.: AIA Press, 1994).
21. Dawn Kawamoto, "Intel Awaits Government Move on Expensing Options," *CNET News*, zdnet.com.com/2100-1103_2-5293683 .html.

6: A Tale of Three Boards

1. See General Corporation Law for the State of Delaware, www.del code.state.de.us/title8/c001/sc04/index.htm#TopOfPage.
2. See, for example, "Board Failed in Its Duty, but Others Must Learn," *Boston Globe*, 4/7/02.
3. Jeffrey L. Cruikshank and David B. Sicilia, *The Engine That Could* (New York: Harvard Business School Press, 1997), pp. 320–21.
4. Cruikshank and Malcolm, *Herman Miller, Inc.*, pp. 22 and 136.
5. Jay W. Lorsch and Elizabeth Maciver, *Pawns or Potentates* (Boston: Harvard Business School Press, 1989).
6. See, for example, "Board Failed in Its Duty."
7. Unless otherwise noted, my WorldCom references come from one of two sources. The first is the "Report of Investigation" by the Special Investigative Committee of the Board of Directors of WorldCom, Inc., 3/31/03, which I'll identify as the SIC report. It's available at news.findlaw.com/hdocs/docs/worldcom/bdspcomm60903rpt.pdf. The second is the "First Interim Report of Dick Thornburgh, Bankruptcy Court Examiner," 11/4/02, which I'll refer to as the FIR. It's available at news.findlaw.com/hdocs/docs/worldcom/thornburgh 1strpt.pdf. Recommended reading, unless you're faint of heart.
8. My two primary sources are "The Role of the Board of Directors in Enron's Collapse," a report prepared by the Permanent Subcommittee on Investigations of the Committee on Governmental Affairs, United States Senate, 7/8/02, which is on the Web at news .findlaw.com/hdocs/docs/enron/senpsi70802rpt.pdf, and "Report

of Investigation by the Special Investigative Committee of the Board of Directors of Enron Corp.," 2/1/02, available at news.findlaw .com/hdocs/docs/enron/sicreport. Unless otherwise noted, all my Enron facts come from these two reports.

9. "Justice Department Expands Charges Against Former Enron CFO Andrew Fastow, Broadband Executives," press release from the Department of Justice, www.usdoj.gov/opa/pr/2003/May/03_crm _268.htm.

10. From a *CNNMoney* press release, 5/7/02, www.cnn.com/money/ 2002/05/07/news/companies/enron_board/.

11. From Jaedicke's "prepared witness testimony" before the House Committee on Energy and Commerce, 2/7/02, energycommerce .house.gov/107/Hearings/02072002hearing485/Jaedicke798print .htm.

12. Bob Jensen, "Enron's Cast of Characters and Their Stock Sales," www.trinity.edu/rjensen/Fraud/EnronCast.htm. These figures don't reflect any transaction costs, so the gains to the individuals were somewhat smaller.

13. From GE's "Notice of 2003 Annual Meeting and Proxy Statement," www.ge.com/jsp/investor/proxy/notice.jsp.

14. Note the phrase "deferred stock units." These DSUs, so called, are not options but rather a form of tracking stock. The units are cashed out upon the director's retirement. "DSUs," explains GE, "more closely align the directors' interests with the long-term interests of shareholders."

15. www.ge.com/en/spotlight/commitment/governance/governance_ principles.htm.

16. Survey results found on the GE Web site, www.ge.com/en/ company/news/gmi_ge_report.htm.

7: Outsourcing and Offshoring

1. *New Yorker,* 8/30/04.

2. Katherine Boo, "The Churn," *New Yorker,* 3/20/04, p. 62. A great article.

3. Ibid., p. 71.

4. "Duke Energy Employee Advocate," www.dukeemployees.com/ legal13.shtml.

5. As of this writing, after Farley lost a motion to dismiss the class action, this lawsuit is still pending.

6. David Barboza, "Taking the Starch Out of an American Icon," *New York Times,* 3/19/00.

7. "Petulant Plutocrat of the Month," in *Too Much,* an on-line "com-

mentary on capping excessive income and wealth," spring 2000,
www.cipa-apex.org/toomuch/00spring/00spring_petulant.html.

8. "Fruit of the Loom Positioned to Emerge from Bankruptcy," *Stitches Magazine,* stitches.com/mag/apparel_fruit_loom_positioned/.

9. "Fruit of the Loom Condemned for 'Disgraceful Behavior,' " ITGLWF press release, 1/24/01, www.itglwf.org/displaydocument .asp?DocType=Press&Index=81&Language=EN.

10. "Berkshire Hathaway Acquires Fruit of the Loom's Apparel Business," *Wearables Business,* 1/1/02, www.wearablesbusiness.com/ mag/apparel_Berkshire_Hathaway_acquires/.

11. "Petulant Pluctocrat of the Month," *Too Much.* The "legal action" reference is from Barboza, "Taking the Starch Out."

12. Boo, "The Churn," p. 71.

13. Shawn Pogatchnik, "Fruit of the Loom Closing Both Irish Plants, Moving Production to Morocco," Associated Press, 9/15/04, ap.tbo.com/ap/breaking/MGBUY8126ZD.html.

14. "Chairman's Letter," Berkshire Hathaway's 2003 annual report, p. 9, www.berkshirehathaway.com/2003ar/impnote03.html.

15. For the contemporary version of CSR, see the *Stanford Social Innovation Review,* www.ssireview.com.

16. This interesting fact is from a PowerPoint presentation entitled "Foundations of Finance, Chapter 6," and apparently is part of the curriculum at the McCombs School at University of Texas. My apologies for not being able to credit the unnamed author, whose work is available at www.mccombs.utexas.edu/faculty/heidi.toprac/ Chapter%206. ppt.

17. See, for example, Mark J. Roe, "The Shareholder Wealth Maximization Norm and Industrial Organization," www.law.harvard.edu/ programs/olin_center/.

18. Jeffrey E. Garten, "Offshoring: You Ain't Seen Nothin' Yet," *BusinessWeek,* 6/21/04, p. 28.

19. Robert Orr, "Offshoring Opens Gap in Financial Services Race," *Financial Times,* 6/29/04.

20. Steve Lohr, "Evidence of High-Skill Work Going Abroad," *New York Times,* 6/16/04.

21. William M. Bulkeley, "IBM to Export Highly Paid Jobs to India, China," *Wall Street Journal,* 12/15/03.

22. Andrew Pollack, "Who's Reading Your X-ray?" *New York Times,* 11/16/03.

23. Dan Ackman, "Outsourcing CEOs Get Big Pay Hikes," *Forbes,* 8/31/04, www.forbes.com/home_asia/compensation/2004/08/31/ cx_da_0831topnews.html.

24. Beth Healy, "High-tech Start-ups Feel Push to Outsource," *Boston*

Globe, 9/23/04, nl.newsbank.com/nl-search/we/Archives?p_action
=doc&p_docid=1054B3411C78FB22&p_docnum=9.

25. Gene Sperling, "The International Economy," *Progressive Politics* (3), 82–88.
26. Joseph Kahn, "Foul Water and Air Part of Cost of the Boom in China's Exports," *New York Times,* 11/4/03.
27. David Whelan, "The Slipper Solution," *Forbes,* 5/24/04, p. 64.
28. David Brooks, "Refuting the Cynics," *New York Times,* 11/25/03. I'm not a cynic, but I definitely don't share Brooks's rosy view of the world.

8: Wal-Mart Nation?

1. See, for example, William Grieder, "A New Giant Sucking Sound," *Nation,* 12/31/01, www.globalpolicy.org/socecon/inequal/labor/ 1231 suck.htm.
2. For an adoring profile of Wal-Mart, see Robert Slater's *The Wal-Mart Decade* (New York: Penguin Books, 2000). For a more straightforward account of the company's history from a strategy standpoint, see Pankaj Ghemawat, Stephen P. Bradley, and Ken Mark, "Wal-Mart Stores in 2003," Harvard Business School case N9-704-430, 9/13/03; available for purchase online at harvardbusinessonline .hbsp.harvard.edu/b02/en/common/item_detail.jhtml?id=704430.
3. And with the advent of "self-checkout," you can now hand your money over to a machine and have no contact with a human whatsoever. And get ready for RFID, or radio frequency identification. Not too far in the future, a transponder in your cart will charge your debit card the minute you put the item in your cart. The march of progress!
4. "Store Watch: Location, Location, Location," Morgan Stanley Equity Research report, 2/7/05.
5. This is the assumption put forward by Simon London, "A Country Within a Country," *Financial Times,* 7/9/04.
6. Ibid.
7. Abigail Goldman and Nancy Cleeland, "The Wal-Mart Effect," *Los Angeles Times,* 11/23/03.
8. Ibid.
9. Kenneth Eskey, "Wal-Mart: The Lovable Store Some Merchants Can Truly Hate," *Seattle Times,* 4/12/92, http://www.p-n-a.org/ WalMart/mompop.html.
10. Edward O. Welles, "When Wal-Mart Comes to Town," *Inc.,* July 1993, pf.inc.com/magazine/19930701/3644.html. For a more recent summary of Stone's work, see Matthew Grim, "Wal-Mart uber Alles," *American Demographics,* 10/1/03, www.findarticles.com/p/

articles/mi_m4021/is_8_25/ni_108538942. Grim describes a "startling swath of destruction" wreaked by Wal-Mart.

11. Albert Norman, "Eight Ways to Beat Wal-Mart," *Nation*, 3/28/94, www.norfolk-country.com/users/claytons/walmart.html.

12. Welles, "When Wal-Mart Comes to Town."

13. Norman, "Eight Ways to Beat Wal-Mart."

14. Donella Meadows, "How to Fight Superstore Sprawl," www .sustainer.org/dbm_archive/search.php?display_article=vn553super storeed.

15. "Bentonville, AR. Annual review: Wal-Mart Realty Has 371 'Darkstores,' " 2/21/04, www.sprawl-busters.com, as quoted in "The Truth About Wal-Mart," www.votenader.org/issues/index.php?cid=47.

16. George F. Will, "Waging War on Wal-Mart," *Newsweek*, 7/5/04, www.msnbc.msn.com/id/5304839/site/newsweek/print/1/display model/1098/.

17. "2004-04-07: Inglewood, CA. Voters Hand Wal-Mart Second Overwhelming Defeat in One Month," www.sprawl-busters.com/search.php?readstory=1396. The "sprawl-busters" Web site is the creation of Albert Norman, who led the original fight against Wal-Mart in Greenfield, Massachusetts.

18. Steven Greenhouse, "Illegally in U.S., and Never a Day Off at Wal-Mart," *New York Times*, 11/5/03.

19. Goldman and Cleeland, "The Wal-Mart Effect."

20. Jeffrey E. Garten, "Wal-Mart Gives Globalism a Bad Name," *BusinessWeek*, 3/8/04, p. 24.

21. "Wal-Mart Stores in 2003," Harvard Business School, p. 15.

22. Ibid.

23. "Organized Labor Recognizing the Threat of Wal-Mart and Sam's Club," United Food and Commercial Workers Union Web site, www.ufcw400.org/news/walmart/workplace.html.

24. "Wal-Mart Stores in 2003," Harvard Business School, p. 16.

25. "The Truth About Wal-Mart," www.votenader.org/issues/index .php?cid=47.

26. Amy Tsao, "The Two Faces of Wal-Mart," *BusinessWeek*, www.businessweek.com:/print/bwdaily/dnflash/jan2004.

27. See the Wal-Mart entry in wordiq.com, www.wordiq.com/definition/Wal-Mart.

28. Drew Hasselback, "Wal-Mart's Free Ride in California?" (Toronto) *Financial Post*, 8/7/04.

29. Froma Harrop, "Wal-Mart's Everyday High Costs," *Providence Journal*, 10/23/03, www.ufcw791.org/031108walmart.html.

30. www.wordiq.com/definition/Wal-Mart.

31. Adam Geller, "As Union Nears Win, Wal-Mart Closes Store," Associ-

ated Press, 2/10/05, www.commondreams.org/headlines05/0210-13
.htm.

32. "Organized Labor Recognizing the Threat of Wal-Mart and Sam's Club," United Food and Commercial Workers Union.

33. From George Palast, *The Best Democracy Money Can Buy* (New York: Plume, 2003), quoted in www.wordiq.com/definition/Wal-Mart.

34. Quoted by Jane Yoder-Short "With Wal-Mart's Purchasing Might, Cheaper Not Always Better," *Iowa City Press-Citizen*, 1/9/04, www.press-citizen.com/opinion/writersgroup/010904yodershort .htm.

35. Goldman and Cleeland, "The Wal-Mart Effect."

36. Jim Hightower, "If Wal-Mart Comes to Your Town, Kill It," *Idaho Observer*, October 2002, www.proliberty.com/observer/20021009 .htm.

37. Ibid.

38. John Helvar, "Costco: The Only Company Wal-Mart Fears," *Fortune*, www.fortune.com/fortune/investing/articles/0,15114,538834, 00.html.

39. Statistics from Daniel Gross, "Shop the Vote," *Slate*, 8/10/04, slate.msn.com/id/2104988/; Christine Frey, "Costco's Love of Labor: Employees' Well-Being Key to Its Success," *Seattle Post-Intelligencer*, 3/29/04, www.seattlepi.nwsource.com/business/166680 costco29.html; and Julie Schmit, "Costco Wins Loyalty with Bulky Bargains," *USA Today*, www.usatoday.com/money/industries/retail/ 2004-09-23-costco_x.htm.

40. Frey, "Costco's Love of Labor."

41. Michelle Conlin and Aaron Bernstein, "Working and Poor," *BusinessWeek*, 5/31/04, p. 61.

42. Schmit, "Costco Wins Loyalty with Bulky Bargains."

43. Stanley Holmes and Wendy Zellner, "The Costco Way," *BusinessWeek*, 4/12/04, www.businessweek.com/magazine/.

44. Schmit, "Costco Wins Loyalty with Bulky Bargains."

45. Holmes and Zellner, "The Costco Way."

46. Kortney Stringer, "Costco's Deep Discounts Don't Extend to Its Share Price," *Wall Street Journal*, 2/22/05.

47. Garten, "Wal-Mart Gives Globalism a Bad Name."

48. Tsao, "The Two Faces of Wal-Mart."

49. "Wal-Mart Stores in 2003," Harvard Business School, p. 16.

50. Holmes and Zellner, "The Costco Way."

51. Tsao, "The Two Faces of Wal-Mart."

9: Putting the Health Back in Health Care

1. Getting paid is more important, of course—right up to the moment when you experience a medical disaster. Then getting paid takes a back seat, sometimes even a distant back seat, to health-care coverage.

2. Statistics from *Health Insurance Coverage in America,* Kaiser Commission on Medicaid and the Uninsured, December 2003.

3. Stephanie Strom, "For Middle Class, Health Insurance Becomes a Luxury," *New York Times,* 11/16/03.

4. Lucette Lagnado, "Hospitals Try Extreme Measures to Collect Their Overdue Debts," *Wall Street Journal,* 10/30/03.

5. Strom, "For Middle Class, Health Insurance Becomes a Luxury."

6. Lagnado, "Hospitals Try Extreme Measures."

7. "Uncharitable Care: How Hospitals Are Gouging and Even Arresting the Uninsured," by the staff of *Democracy Now!,* Common Dreams News Center Web site, www.commondreams.org/headslines04/0108-07.htm.

8. Julie Appleby, "Hospitals Sock Uninsured with Much Bigger Bills," *USA Today,* www.usatoday.com/money/industries/health/2004-02-24-hospital-bills_x.htm.

9. Lucette Lagnado, "HHS Chief Scolds Hospitals for Their Treatment of Uninsured," *Wall Street Journal,* 2/20/04.

10. Dan Roberts and Ellen Kelleher, "Alternative Therapy: U.S. Companies Search for Radical Ways to Cut the Spiraling Cost of Employee Healthcare," *Financial Times,* 3/19/04.

11. Ezekial J. Emanuel and Victor R. Fuchs, "The Universal Cure," *New York Times,* 11/18/03.

12. Regina E. Herzlinger, "Let's Put Consumers in Charge of Health Care," *Harvard Business Review,* July 2002.

13. Ibid.

14. Amy Snow Landa, "AMA Major Force in Federal Lobbying," www.ama-assn.org/amednews/2001/10/15/gvsd1015.htm.

15. Maureen Glabman, "Lobbyists That the Founders Never Dreamed Of," *Managed Care,* August 2002, www.managedcaremag.com/archives/0208/0208.lobbying.html.

16. Emanuel and Fuchs, "The Universal Cure."

17. Herzlinger, "Let's Put Consumers in Charge of Health Care."

18. Roberts and Kelleher, "Alternative Therapy."

19. "IHA Pay for Performance California Initiative Evaluates 215 Medical Groups for Reward and Recognition by Health Plans," press release from IHA, 8/9/04, www.iha.org/080904.htm.

20. This section is largely derived from Vanessa Fuhrmans, "Higher Co-pays May Take Toll on Health," *Wall Street Journal,* 5/19/04.

21. Ibid.

22. Zachary Bromer, "Domestic Partner Benefits," *Salary,* www.salary
    .com/benefits/layouthmls/bnfl_display_nocat_Ser78_Par167.html.
23. "Domestic Partner Benefits: Facts and Background," Employee Ben-
    efit Research Institute, March 2004.
24. The advent of legally sanctioned gay marriages and civil unions,
    however, is beginning to change this whole calculation.
25. Bromer, "Domestic Partner Benefits." It should be noted too that
    some states—like Virginia—actually prohibit insurance companies
    based in those states from providing benefits to domestic partners.
26. "Winning Domestic Partner Benefits," a Human Rights Campaign
    Foundation Q&A, www.hrc.org/TemplateRedirect.cfm?template=/
    ContentManagement/ContentDisplay.cfm&ContentID=10790.
27. "Employers Cutting Domestic Partner Benefits After Gay Wed-
    dings," www.boston.com/business/articles/2004/04/28employers
    _cutting_domestic_partner_benefits_after_gay_weddings/. Ironically,
    the legalization of gay marriages in Massachusetts has led Beth
    Israel/Deaconess (among other organizations) to *drop* domestic part-
    ner coverage on the grounds that same-sex couples can now qualify
    for health care through marriage, and that this antidiscrimination
    remedy is no longer needed. Stay tuned!
28. Jan Gleason, "First Year of Domestic Partner Benefits Runs
    Smoothly," www.emory.edu/EMORY_REPORT/erarchive/1996/
    October/ERoct.7/10_7_96first_year.html.
29. "Home Depot Announces Domestic Partner Health Insurance After
    HRC Reveals Pets Already Covered," a Human Rights Campaign
    Foundation press release, 9/2/04, www.hrc.org/Template Redirect
    .cfm?template=/ContentManagement/ContentDisplay.cfm&Content
    ID=22583.
30. Roberts and Kelleher, "Alternative Therapy."

10: The CEO Checklist

1. "Our Hidden History: Corporations in America," www.reclaim
   democracy.org.
2. For a truly interesting account of this episode, see Thom Hartmann,
   "The Theft of Human Rights," www.thomhartmann.com/thest
   .shtml.
3. Quoted in "Our Hidden History."
4. Rich Teerlink and Lee Ozley, *More than a Motorcycle* (Boston: HBS
   Press, 2000), p. 268.
5. Joe Klein, "Jane Swift: No More Governor Mom," www.time.com/
   time/columnist/klein/article/0,9565,219749,00.html.
6. "Donaldson Laments US Chiefs' Lack of Ethical Leadership," *Financial Times,* 9/20/04.

7. "Herb Kelleher, the Complete Interview," www.mccombs.utexas .edu/news/pressreleases/kelleher_int03.asp.

8. By most reasonable calculations, Jones generated a slightly higher annual earnings growth rate at GE than did his much-lauded successor.

9. Frank Batten, *The Weather Channel* (Boston: HBS Press, 2002), p. 234.

10. "The Buck Stops Here," from an explanation of Harry Truman's desk sign, www.trumanlibrary.org/buckstop.htm.

11. Raymond H. Geselbracht, "Harry Truman, Poker Player," www.archives.gov/publications/prologue/spring_2003_truman_ poker.html.

12. www.trumanlibrary.org/buckstop.htm.

13. Peter M. Senge and Katrin H. Käufer, "Communities of Leaders or No Leadership at All," abridged for publication in Barbara Kellerman and Larraine R. Matusak, *Cutting Edge Leadership 2000,* www.ohrd.wisc.edu/WSTC/wstc_2004/readings/Communities%20 of%20Leaders.pdf.

14. Arthur Levitt Jr., "The Imperial CEO Is No More," *Wall Street Journal,* 3/17/05.

INDEX

LEO HINDERY, JR., is Managing Partner of InterMedia Partners, a major private equity firm. Prior to starting InterMedia Partners, Hindery was CEO of the YES Network, the nation's premier regional sports network, which he helped form in the summer of 2001 as the television home of the New York Yankees and the New Jersey Nets. Previously he has been Chairman and CEO of Global-Center Inc., President and CEO of AT&T Broadband, and President and CEO of TeleCommunications, Inc. (TCI). Hindery is the author of *The Biggest Game of All*. He lives in New York City.